AWAITING THE MANGER

OCIEANNA
FLEISS

HARVEST HOUSE PUBLISHERS
EUGENE, OREGON

Published in association with the literary agency of The Steve Laube Agency, LLC, 24 W. Camelback Rd. A635, Phoenix, Arizona 85013.

Cover designed by Faceout Studio, Molly von Borstel

Cover and interior images © Romanova Ekaterina, Studio_G, Filmaks / Shutterstock

Interior designed by Chad Dougherty

For bulk, special sales, or ministry purchases, please call 1-800-547-8979. Email: Customerservice@hhpbooks.com

Awaiting the Manger

Copyright © 2023 by Ocieanna Fleiss
Published by Harvest House Publishers
Eugene, Oregon 97408
www.harvesthousepublishers.com

ISBN 978-0-7369-8778-3 (Hardcover)
ISBN 978-0-7369-8779-0 (eBook)

Printed in Colombia

23 24 25 26 27 28 29 30 31 / NI / 10 9 8 7 6 5 4 3 2 1

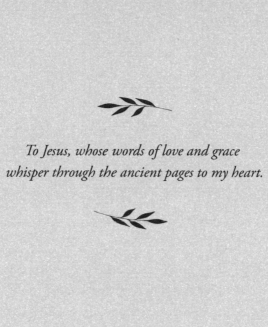

To Jesus, whose words of love and grace
whisper through the ancient pages to my heart.

Not to us, O LORD, not to us, but to your name give glory,
for the sake of your steadfast love and your faithfulness!

PSALM 115:1

The Scriptures are like the swaddling clothes of the
holy child Jesus; unroll them, and there you find your
Savior. The essence of the Word of God is Christ.

CHARLES SPURGEON

Beginning with Moses and all the Prophets, he
interpreted to them in all the
Scriptures the things concerning himself.

LUKE 24:27

CONTENTS

INTRODUCTION

*Behold, the virgin shall conceive and bear a
son, and shall call his name Immanuel.*

ISAIAH 7:14

Instead of jumping into the chaos the Christmas season often brings, I'd like to invite you to relish these 25 days of Advent. While you wait for the celebration of Jesus's birth, join me in reflecting, listening, and watching for him.

In Isaiah 7:14, God tells us that the Messiah will be called Immanuel. (We'll explore the moment when God proclaimed this name in chapter 21.) Immanuel—Jesus—is the one I set my eyes on during this season. Why?

Immanuel means "God with us," and it is the name of God that whispers my personal story. I was separated from God—sinful, damaged, unable to enter his holy presence—but because of a love greater than I can grasp, the walls barring me from him collapsed. A Savior, gentle in a manger, glorious in his brokenness—with blood-stained brow, ripped hands and feet—climbed through the rubble to rescue me.

Is this your story too? It's a story woven over millennia in true tales etched by prophets and poets on stone and papyrus, then preserved for us in what we call the Old Testament. Here we find the shining face of the baby in the hay. In those old stories he was there, as present with us as he has always been and will always remain.

Awaiting the Manger pauses to peek at the hints of Jesus's coming from heaven to earth whispered throughout the ancient pages of Scripture. Echoing from the deep past, thundering in ever greater clarity, we will watch the declaration of love trumpeted about on Christmas morning and know more deeply the Savior who did not leave us as orphans but came to us in love and grace.

I sit in humble anticipation as we begin this journey together, in awe of the majestic depth of God's Word, and overflowing with excitement for the encouragement that awaits.

A WORD ABOUT THE TEXT

Oh, how I love Scripture! It's God's holy Word, breathed from him to us. It is the normal way he speaks to us, and the Bible reveals all we need to know of who God is—imagine that!

To be honest, I tremble when I teach from Scripture and even more when I write about it. I deeply desire to honor God by first painstakingly studying the passages, and then choosing with care the words I use to communicate God's story to you. In *Awaiting the Manger*, as I retell Scripture stories, I do take the liberty to "put flesh on the bones," as my pastor friend calls it. At times, in order to give a fresh perspective, you'll experience the story through one of the characters' points of view. Other times I'll use credible historical details to paint the scene. And in a few spots, I'll imagine a scenario that could have happened. Weaving through the stories, I strive to add only plausible details, based in research of the biblical text, the time period, and the language, but these parts are *not* the Word of God! As you read each chapter, I urge you to read the Scripture passages (found in the "Read" section), as well as examine the references run in the text, to hear what God is saying for yourself.

A WORD ABOUT THE HYMNS

At the end of each day's devotional, I've listed an Advent or Christmas hymn for you and your family to enjoy. If you're unfamiliar with the melody, feel free to search the internet for a version you like. Another option is to simply read the words of the hymn. They are rich and flowing with encouragement.

"Yes," said Queen Lucy. "In our world too,
a stable once had something inside it that
was bigger than our whole world."

LUCY PEVENSIE,
The Last Battle by C.S. Lewis

1

BEFORE THE BEGINNING

He chose us in him before the foundation of the world.

EPHESIANS 1:4

When did the story of Jesus begin? When the angel Gabriel descended to the dusty town of Nazareth to find a peasant girl who would be blessed among women? Or did it begin earlier in history's halls? Maybe in an easily skimmed-over verse from the book of Micah, when the prophet hailed the little town of Bethlehem as the birthplace of the Messiah. Perhaps it was when Isaiah's aged hands scribbled down the Holy Spirit's description of a child born "unto us" who would be stricken, smitten, and afflicted (Isaiah 53:4).

Or was it further back into the dark past when our first parents Adam and Eve sided against God, turned their hearts to the serpent, and broke the commandment to not eat from the forbidden tree? Or maybe shortly after this, when God promised a Deliverer would come from the seed of the woman to crush the serpent's head, restoring the shattered relationship between God and his sons and daughters? (Genesis 3:15). Surely that was when the story began.

But no. Not even then.

Jesus's story—the story of our deliverance from the shackles of sin to new life—began here: "Even as he chose us in him before the foundation of the world" (Ephesians 1:4).

Before the universe was created, back in the pre-creation womb that our minds fail to fathom—yes, way back then—he loved us. No space, no stars, no planets, no Earth. The Spirit wasn't moving over the waters—there were no waters. Before the molecules of life connected, or a neuron vibrated, or blood pumped through a heart valve. All that existed was the perfect union of love amid the Godhead—Father, Son, Holy Spirit. Three in one. Holiness, love, creativity.

And there, before time and space, he thought of us. The next verse says, "In love he predestined us" (Ephesians 1:4-5).

During this mysterious age, the Father, Son, and Holy Spirit made a divine promise—the Immanuel promise—that Jesus would dwell among us (John 1:14). He would heal the sick with a word or touch or spit. He would restore the outcasts. He would speak redemption to the broken bride who ventured to a well on a hot afternoon (John 4:1-45). He would refuse to condemn the woman caught in adultery, sparing her from being stoned to death by self-righteous Pharisees (John 8:1-11). He would remove the shackles of the demon-possessed, cave-bound man, replacing his torment with peace (Mark 5:1-20). He would weep with sisters and raise a brother (John 11:1-44). He would cry to his Abba Father in a garden, alone (Matthew 26:36-46). When the time came, he would walk the ugly road to the cross, paved with thorns and mockery and lashings (Matthew 27:27-31). On a dark Friday, he would drink the full cup of his Father's wrath (Matthew 27:46)—and on a bright Sunday he would rise in glorious victory (1 Corinthians 15:4).

And, all of this would first be heralded in a tiny space crammed into a crowded town, when, begotten of the Father's love, the Son would trade his throne for a manger (Luke 2:7).

A lot happened before the beginning.

Artist and saint alike grope in awe to comprehend…the Master of the Universe, become of earth, earthy, in order to be one with his creatures so that we may be one with him.

MADELEINE L'ENGLE

God loved us before the stars twinkled, but "knowing" his love eludes us at times. Today, speak of his ancient and unbreakable love to yourself and those around you. (Ephesians 3:19)

What response do you have to knowing that before the beginning, God chose to love you? If you really grasped that he cherishes you, how would your thoughts, words, and actions change? (Zephaniah 3:17; Jeremiah 31:3; 1 John 4:19)

Father, before the foundation of the world you knew me, you loved me. Awaken me to rest in the knowledge of your eternal love.

Ephesians 1

SING

OF THE FATHER'S LOVE BEGOTTEN

Translation by J.M. Neale (1851), extended by Henry W. Baker (1861)

Of the Father's love begotten
Ere the worlds began to be,
He is Alpha and Omega,
He the Source, the Ending he,
Of the things that are, that have been,
And that future years shall see,
Evermore and evermore!

O that birth forever blessed,
When the Virgin, full of grace,
By the Holy Ghost conceiving,
Bore the Savior of our race;
And the babe, the world's Redeemer,
First revealed his sacred face,
Evermore and evermore!

This is he whom heav'n-taught singers
Sang of old with one accord,
Whom the Scriptures of the prophets
Promised in their faithful word;
Now he shines, the long-expected;
Let creation praise its Lord,
Everymore and evermore!

O ye heights of heav'n, adore him;
Angel hosts, his praises sing;
All dominions, bow before him,
And extol our God and King;
Let no tongue on earth be silent,
Ev'ry voice in concert ring,
Evermore and evermore

Christ, to thee, with God the Father,
And, O Holy Ghost, to thee,
I Iymn, and chant, and high thanksgiving,
And unwearied praises be,
Honor, glory, and dominion,
And eternal victory,
Evermore and evermore.

2

THE WOMAN'S OFFSPRING

I am sure that neither death nor life, nor angels nor rulers, nor things present nor things to come, nor powers, nor height nor depth, nor anything else in all creation, will be able to separate us from the love of God in Christ Jesus our Lord.

ROMANS 8:38-39

For a while, Adam and Eve lived and breathed and had their being in joyful wonder with their God, relishing the sapphire skies, delighting in the giraffes and hedgehogs and blue jays, feasting on the harvest of pomegranates and figs. Blanketed in their Father's love, they were naked and unafraid. They existed in joyful union with their Creator—perfect submission, perfect delight.

But into this safe temple, the serpent trespassed, seducing them into eating from the one tree the Father had commanded his children to avoid. Even though our first parents had lived in the light of God's favor, Adam and Eve chose to change sides. They believed the lie that God didn't love them enough, that he had selfishly withheld something from them. So they ate of the forbidden tree.

And then they died. Life is love and communion with the Lord (John 17:3). So with that first bite, Adam and Eve were spiritually dead in their trespasses and sins (Colossians 2:13). Dead as in no life. No heartbeat. No will.

Their lovely, intimate fellowship with God was gone. Two dead ones could not restore it. With death came fear. Still naked, they were now afraid of being seen, for the Judge of the universe found them in sin. And the consequence was great—God banished them from the garden. East, away from the circle of "God with us," never to return, and he sent angels with flaming swords to block the entrance. Who could possibly break through those deadly swords? Who could endure the savage death that would come to anyone who tried? Could fellowship with God be restored?

Only God could repair the broken fellowship, and we first glimpse his rescue plan in these words he spoke to the serpent, "I will put enmity between you and the woman, and between your offspring and her offspring; he shall bruise your head, and you shall bruise his heel" (Genesis 3:15).

In these puzzling words, we find the whisper of a promise. Someday—tomorrow? Next week? Far in the future? Adam and Eve didn't know when, but they did know that through his suffering, he would free them from the doom of hopeless wandering. They would walk with their Father once again.

But that was all they knew.

Send him soon, I imagine Eve prayed as she left the garden. *Yes, soon Lord.*

Millenia passed, and then, to a daughter of Eve an angel came. This angel was unlike those who wielded the flaming swords blocking entrance to the Father's presence—instead, this angel announced the way to be with God again. "Greetings, O favored one, the Lord is with you" (Luke 1:28).

Did you see that? The Immanuel promise was right there in the greeting. "The Lord is with you." Finally! Finally, he would arrive—the one who would crush the serpent's head, endure the fiery sword, and usher us into sweet fellowship once again.

Yet, thy compassions yearn over me,
thy heart hastens to my rescue,
thy love endured my curse,
thy mercy bore my deserved stripes.

TRADITIONAL PURITAN PRAYER
The Valley of Vision, **Arthur Bennett (Editor)**

Doubts, shame, greed, lust, gossip, deceit—merely a few of the weapons the Enemy craftily tempts us with. These are too strong for us to resist on our own. We must cry out to Jesus, and he will crush the serpent's influence in our life, day by day.

In what areas of your life have you taken sides against Jesus? How can you practice surrendering those areas to Christ? (Colossians 3:1-17)

Long-awaited Savior, as the days draw closer to the celebration of your birth, please speak peace to my heart and let your mercy resound within a fallen world that desperately needs saving.

READ

Genesis 1–3

SING

COMFORT, COMFORT YE MY PEOPLE

Johannes Olearius (1671); translated by Catherine Winkworth (1863)

Comfort, comfort ye my people,
Speak ye peace, thus saith our God;
Comfort those who sit in darkness,
Mourning 'neath their sorrow's load.
Speak ye to Jerusalem
Of the peace that waits for them;
Tell her that her sins I cover,
And her warfare now is over.

Yea, her sins our God will pardon,
Blotting out each dark misdeed;
All that well deserved his anger
He no more will see or heed.
She hath suffered many a day
Now her griefs have passed away;
God will change her pining sadness
Into ever-springing gladness.

For the herald's voice is crying
In the desert far and near,
Biding all men to repentance,
Since the kingdom now is here.
O that warning cry obey!
Now prepare for God a way;
Let the valleys rise to meet him,
And the hills bow down to greet him.

Make ye straight what long was crooked,
Make the rougher places plain;
Let your hearts be true and humble,
As befits his holy reign.
For the glory of the Lord
Now o'er earth is shed abroad;
And all flesh shall see the token,
That his word is never broken.

3

NOAH'S HIDING PLACE

You have died, and your life is hidden with Christ in God.

COLOSSIANS 3:3

After a long day working on the ark, Noah settled into his steps, knowing he walked with God. Across the world, humankind had rebelled against the Lord, acting in treacherous, wicked ways. Yet God had given Noah grace, a grace that forged an unquenchable desire within him to trust and serve his Lord.

In obedience, Noah and his family of eight went to sleep each night with bodies sore from building the ark to God's detailed specifications. But worse than the physical toll was the endless mocking from his neighbors...*Am I a fool for believing this, God?* he wondered. The rest of the world went about their lives, planting, sowing, reaping. They didn't know—or perhaps didn't believe—that it was their last winter festival, last spring flowers, last summer heat, last harvest. Noah gazed to the fields and then outward, upward to the hills and mountains. *Would water really fill the earth?*

Yet, each morning Noah returned to the ark, palming the curved gopher wood, counting the cubits with his hand, breathing in the wood particles. As the evening's campfire burned, Noah prayed as he gazed at the expansive, starry sky.

By God's grace, Noah persevered in obedient faith while the mass of humanity persevered in arrogant self-determination. Even when the rain pounded, melting the dusty earth into mud, unbelieving laughter drowned out the sounds of Noah's prophetic warnings. As the floods rose, however, intense fear finally flooded the hearts of the wicked. But it was too late. God closed the door of the ark, and the Almighty's judgment destroyed all living things. "Everything on the dry land in whose nostrils was the breath of life died" (Genesis 7:22).

Water covered the earth as it had before God's words brought light to creation. In his holy anger, the Lord condemned his glorious creation to its original state—watery darkness, formless and void.

Yet God's steadfast love endured. He never forgot the promise to Adam and Eve of a Deliverer, and he didn't destroy the seed of humanity. Hidden in the ark, Noah and his sons, Ham, Shem, and Japheth, and their wives, survived in safety. Through them came a new beginning. And through their descendants, over hundreds and thousands of years, finally…"When the fullness of time had come, God sent forth his Son, born of woman" (Galatians 4:6).

When God rescued Noah from the flood, he also rescued Christmas. Father Noah had to survive in a wooden boat so his greater Son Jesus could be placed in a wooden manger and die on a wooden cross to drown in the tide of God's judgment—so we wouldn't have to. So we too could be hidden, not in an ark, but safe in the arms of the Savior.

I believe only and alone in the service of Jesus Christ. In him is all refuge and solace.

JOHANNES KEPLER

If God has you safely in his care, there is nothing to fear.
Ask him to help you trust him.

What storms are you battling? What would it look like for you to
hide in Christ till they pass? (Psalm 46:1-3; 119:113-117)

My refuge, my Lord, let me hide myself in you.

Genesis 6–9

SEE AMID THE WINTER SNOW
Edward Caswall (1851)

See, amid the winter's snow,
Born for us on earth below,
See the tender Lamb appears,
Promised from eternal years.

Refrain:
Hail, thou ever blessed morn!
Hail, redemption's happy dawn!
Sing through all Jerusalem,
Christ is born in Bethlehem.

Lo, within a manger lies
He who built the starry skies:
He who, throned in height sublime,
Sits amid the cherubim.[Refrain]

Say, ye holy shepherds, say—
What your joyful news today?
Wherefore have ye left your sheep
On the lonely mountain steep? [Refrain]

"As we watched at dead of night,
Lo! We saw a wondrous light;
Angels singing, peace on earth,
Told us of the Savior's birth." [Refrain]

Sacred infant, all divine,
What a tender love was thine,
Thus to come from highest bliss
Down to such a world as this! [Refrain]

Teach, O teach us, holy child,
By thy face so meek and mild,
Teach us to resemble thee,
In thy sweet humility. [Refrain]

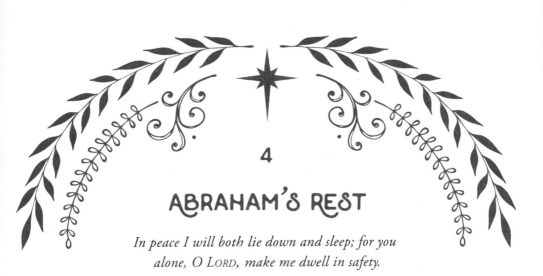

4

ABRAHAM'S REST

In peace I will both lie down and sleep; for you
alone, O LORD, make me dwell in safety.

PSALM 4:8

Soft breaths. Closed eyes. Relaxed muscles. The implicit trust that no harm will come. Sleep. This is the state God put Abraham into when he inaugurated the next element in his plan to save the world.

The stars were beginning to peek through the darkening sky when God came to Abraham. Yes, God himself. And just in time. Abraham was agitated. He longed for answers. Years earlier, God had promised that Abraham would be "the father of a multitude of nations" (Genesis 17:4). But like the evening sky, Abraham had also receded into his own twilight, and still no baby moved in Sarah's womb. He hadn't yet fathered an heir, much less a great nation.

The silence of God screamed to his unsettled heart. He craved certainty. Tired of fitful nights—wondering, doubting—he boldly cried out, "O Lord GOD, what will you give me, for I continue childless" (Genesis 15:2). And finally, God gave him a sign.

As darkness edged closer, God told Abraham to kill a heifer, a goat, and a ram, and to cut them in half and lay them out. He was also to find a pigeon and a turtledove—animals fit for sacrifice.

As Abraham performed this bloody, terrifying task, he knew what God was demanding, what halved animals represented to the nations around him. When a great king conquered a lesser king, they would split animals in a ceremony to ratify an agreement. Then the lesser king—humiliated into obedience after being tortured and mocked by the conquering nation—would walk between the torn animals. With this action, the lesser king said, "If I ever break my promises to you, you will thrash me to pieces like these animals."[1]

Despite God's command to not be afraid, Abraham's hands trembled as ravens circled overhead. And with every violent slash, his understanding grew. God was the greater King. Abraham was a mere man. He must try to be faithful, to obey all God asked of him. But he had failed before. If he again fell to temptation, the torn animals shouted his fate.

But then God altered the narrative.

Rather than making him walk between the animals, God put Abraham into a deep sleep, and then did something no great king would ever dream of doing. "When the sun had gone down and it was dark, behold, a smoking fire pot and a flaming torch passed between these pieces" (Genesis 15:17). The fire pot and the flaming torch represented God himself. God—not the lesser king, not just the *greater* king, but the *greatest* King—walked the bloody path through the ripped pieces.

What did Abraham think when he woke up, saw the animals, and knew God had walked between them in his place? What kind of God was this? What kind of kingdom?

Imagine the infant Christ resting in Mary's arms. The Savior of the world's soft breaths, closed eyes, and relaxed muscles exemplified his trust that no harm would come. But years later, after an agonizing night when weariness shut the eyes of his closest friends, Jesus himself would be broken, just like

Abraham's cut animals. Exhausted and alone as darkness fell over the earth, he kept the oath made to Abraham and to us.

Our greatest King knew we would fail. He knew sin would destroy us. And he walked that bloody path of the cross to take the penalty for our sin (1 Corinthians 15:3). Amazingly, in doing so, he brought us rest (Matthew 11:28-30). We can rest in our Father's arms just as Abraham rested in God's, and Jesus rested in Mary's, confident that no harm will come.

You have made us for yourself, O Lord, and
our heart is restless until it rests in you.

AUGUSTINE OF HIPPO

PRACTICE

Thank Jesus for walking the bloody path in your place. How can you walk in humble obedience to the one who gave himself for you?

REFLECT

What are some ways you can learn to rest in what Christ has done for you? What burdens can you lay down that he has already carried? (Exodus 14:14; Psalm 46:10; Mark 6:31)

PRAY

You, O Christ, are my rest. Replace my striving with your peace. Replace my anxiety with your love. Replace my self-reliance with your strength.

READ

Genesis 14

SING

SILENT NIGHT

Joseph Mohr (1816); translated by John Freeman Young (1859)

Silent night! Holy night!
All is calm, all is bright
Round yon virgin mother and Child.
Holy infant, so tender and mild,
Sleep in heavenly peace.
Sleep in heavenly peace.

Silent night! Holy night!
Son of God, love's pure light
Radiant beams from thy holy face,
With the dawn of redeeming grace,
Jesus, Lord at thy birth
Jesus, Lord at thy birth

Silent night! Holy night!
Shepherds quake at the sight!
Glories stream from heav'n afar,
Heavenly hosts sing: Alleluia,
Christ, the Savior is born!
Christ, the Savior is born!

5

HAGAR'S CRY

I will seek the lost, and I will bring back the strayed, and I will bind up the injured, and I will strengthen the weak, and the fat and the strong I will destroy. I will feed them in justice.

EZEKIEL 34:16

Her lips chapping, her feet throbbing, her back aching, Hagar finally staggered to the spring in the desert.

As a young woman, she'd been taken from the arms of her family in lush Egypt. She'd ended up living in Canaan with a bearded man who spoke of a God she'd never seen—not Isis or even the mighty sun god Ra. She'd worked her soft hands hard for Sarah, the lady of the camp. She hated her low position, and she knew she'd never rise to be the mistress herself.

But then dissatisfaction blew through her master and mistress's tents, hot and thick and troublesome like a sandstorm. Over days and weeks, it swelled, agitating Abraham and Sarah. What caused the unrest? Hagar had overheard an argument, but she must have not heard correctly. Sarah accused Abraham's God of not delivering on his promise of a child. A child? Sarah was an old woman. Surely, she wasn't expecting to conceive.

The tension grew until one day Abraham approached Hagar with a surprising plan. She would be his wife.

"Me?" She gaped at the old man, her mistress's husband. Could she marry him? Did she have a choice? She rubbed her arms and felt the rough fabric of a slave's dress. If she married the lord of the family, what would her life be like? Surely, better! More food, a better tent, finer clothing.

After they were wed, she did receive her hoped-for benefits, yet, she always remained lower than Sarah. The matriarch had grown jealous of her relationship with Abraham, and she treated Hagar with harsh words, spiteful glares, and extra chores. How tired Hagar grew of doing the sour woman's bidding!

But then, thankfully, a child grew in her belly. Finally, Hagar had risen above barren Sarah's position. Now, she could repay the unfair treatment she'd received. "She began to despise her mistress" (Genesis 16:4 NIV). For a while, her built-up contempt flooded their encampment like the hot rain that overflowed the Nile in the fall. She acted out her bitterness, biting like an asp. But when Sarah complained to her husband, Abraham gave Sarah permission to treat Hagar "however she liked." Hagar's newfound status toppled like a torndown statue. And Sarah was more brutal than ever.

And so Hagar fled.

Sitting next to the spring, Hagar wiped a tear. Why hadn't Abraham protected her? *Is this how my husband's God wanted me to be treated?* She had fled to the desert and headed south, toward Egypt—toward home.

Touching her bulging belly, doubt about her plan crept in. A pregnant woman, rejected by her community, trudging alone through the bleak wilderness, how could she possibly survive all the way to Egypt? But she couldn't return to Sarah's contempt, nor could she face Abraham's indifference.

Though she wandered by herself, this young slave wife was not alone. Another Traveler, one who would also flee to Egypt 2,000 years later, saw her in that vast desert and came to her. "The angel of the LORD found her by a spring of water in the wilderness, the spring on the way to Shur" (Genesis 16:7). Many theologians think the "angel of the Lord" who came to Hagar was Christ himself.[1] His words were difficult. "Return to your mistress," he said, "and submit to her" (Genesis 16:9). God called Hagar to face the person she most feared. But this time, she knew she was not alone. The Lord loved Hagar too much to let her return to Egypt's idols. And he would bless her with a son. "You shall call his name Ishmael, because the LORD has listened to your affliction" (Genesis 16:11). He saw her. He listened.

Just as he saw Hagar's abandonment, Jesus still sees the desperate state of his people. He listens to our sorrows and afflictions despite how we so helplessly flee from him. He came on that precious morning of the first Christmas, not to condemn the world, but to save it (John 3:17). He sees us. He won't desert us. Like Hagar, in wonder we cry, "I have now seen the One who sees me" (Genesis 16:13 NIV).

You thought you were being made into a decent little cottage but He is building a palace. He intends to come and live in it Himself.

C.S. LEWIS, *Mere Christianity*

PRACTICE

God listened to Hagar. God saw Hagar. Every day during this Advent season, when you wake, remind yourself that he listens to you. Be comforted by the knowledge that he sees you.

REFLECT

Does it ever feel as if God is absent from certain areas of your life?
Which ones? How can you reconcile your feelings of neglect
with the truth of his presence and care?
(Psalm 42; Matthew 28:19; Hebrews 13:5)

PRAY

*O God who sees, thank you for coming to rescue me from the desert of my
sin and misery. Thank you for never leaving me even when I am treated
as if I'm worthless. Thank you for being my strength when I am weak.*

READ

Genesis 16

SING

WHAT CHILD IS THIS?
William Chatterton Dix (1865)

What child is this, who, laid to rest, on Mary's lap is sleeping?
Whom angels greet with anthems sweet, while shepherds watch are keeping?
This, this is Christ the King, whom shepherds guard and angels sing;
Haste, haste to bring him laud, the babe, the son of Mary.

Why lies he in such mean estate, where ox and ass are feeding?
Good Christian, fear; for sinners here the silent Word is pleading.

Nails, spear, shall pierce him through; the cross be borne for me, for you:
Hail, hail the Word made flesh, the babe, the son of Mary.

So bring him incense, gold, and myrrh; come, peasant, king, to own him;
The King of kings salvation brings, let loving hearts enthrone him.
Raise, raise the song on high, the Virgin sings her lullaby;
Joy, joy for Christ is born, the babe, the son of Mary.

6

SARAH'S LAUGHTER

Wait for the LORD; be strong, and let your
heart take courage; wait for the LORD!

PSALM 27:14

The sun's midday heat seeped into Sarah's aged bones as she sat in her tent's door with her husband. *Just a short rest,* she thought. *A breath.* She closed her eyes until the sound of Abraham's movement grabbed her attention. Three mysterious men were approaching, and Abraham was running toward them. Running? *His old legs haven't moved that fast in years.* Then, down to the dusty earth he bowed before them.

They weren't mere men, she realized. One was the Lord. She stiffened. *Come to make another false promise?* Many years ago when he first called them from their home in Ur, God had promised a great nation would come from Abraham (Genesis 12). And again, on that night when Abraham cut the animals, he'd promised an heir (Genesis 15). None of his promises had come true. *What will the Lord promise this time?* Despite her cynicism, a wave of reverent fear struck her heart.

Abraham invited them to stay, so Sarah worked the dough into bread as their finest lamb roasted over the fire. She moved inside the tent and listened as they ate.

The Lord said, "I will surely return to you about this time next year, and Sarah your wife shall have a son" (Genesis 18:10). Abraham was ninety-nine. Sarah eighty-nine. Her womb was long dead, and in a burst of disbelief, she laughed. God heard her faithless chuckles, yet again he spoke his promise. "Is anything too hard for the Lord?" (Genesis 18:14).

Reminded of the holy presence before her, she tried to take it back. "I did not laugh." But she couldn't fool God (Genesis 18:15). He knew the doubt, the disenchantment, the distrust that had hardened in her over the decades.

As weeks turned into months, Sarah's belly slowly grew until finally the doubtful thoughts shifted to seeds of hope. *Maybe there really is life inside me.*

Twenty-five long years after God first spoke the promise to Abraham, the baby was born! Sarah's dead womb brought forth life.

Back in Genesis 3:15, God spoke the first gospel promise—a person, a seed, would come from the woman. Not just 25 years, but millennia passed waiting for the deliverer to arrive.

At the right time, once again a woman was told, "You shall bear a son" (Luke 1:31). This woman was a young virgin, but she and Sarah had something in common—only a miracle could explain the impossible buds of life that blossomed within them.

"How can this be?" Mary asked. But unlike Sarah, Mary believed. Maybe she remembered God's words to her matriarch. "Is anything too hard for the Lord?" (Genesis 18:14). As weeks turned into months, Mary's belly grew.

And finally, the serpent crusher—who would himself someday be crushed—arrived, for despite our snickers and doubts, and usually after a long time of waiting, our Promise Giver always keeps his promises.

I find the doing of the will of God leaves me
no time for disputing about His plans.

GEORGE MACDONALD

When times of waiting come, trusting Jesus sometimes seems impossible; but when we cling to his words, the doubts fly away. Pray for help to trust.

Describe a time of waiting when you struggled to trust.
How can you trust the Lord instead of your own understanding?
(Psalm 62:8; Proverbs 3:5-6)

Heavenly Father, where impatience worries my heart, grant me hope
that in waiting on you, I will find strength to follow, courage to face a
broken world, and grace to serve.

Genesis 18

COME, THOU LONG-EXPECTED JESUS

Charles Wesley (1744)

Come, thou long-expected Jesus,
Born to set thy people free;
From our fears and sins release us;
Let us find our rest in thee.
Israel's strength and consolation,
Hope of all the earth thou art;
Dear Desire of ev'ry nation,
Joy of every longing heart.

Born thy people to deliver,
Born a child, and yet a King,
Born to reign in us forever,
Now thy gracious kingdom bring.
By thine own eternal Spirit
Rule in all our hearts alone;
By thine all-sufficient merit
Raise us to thy glorious throne.

7

ISAAC'S NEAR SACRIFICE

*I have been crucified with Christ. It is no longer I
who live, but Christ who lives in me. And the life
I now live in the flesh I live by faith in the Son of
God, who loved me and gave himself for me.*

GALATIANS 2:20

The turbulent days of Abraham's life seemed to be over—those telling-tall-tales-in-Egypt days, those marrying-your-wife's-maidservant days, those sending-away-your-firstborn-son days (Genesis 12–21). The promised child had finally come from Sarah's dead womb, just as God said he would! Abraham had reason to trust a God who had patiently blessed him, despite an old man's follies.

Years of respite surely awaited him. But God broke into Abraham's time of rest with a commission. "Take your son, your only son Isaac, whom you love, and go to the land of Moriah, and offer him there as a burnt offering on one of the mountains of which I shall tell you" (Genesis 22:2).

And this time he didn't question God. He didn't concoct a way out of it. He didn't listen to anyone but the Lord.

With Mount Moriah looming in the distance, Abraham's old, aching legs trudged beside two servants, a laden donkey, and his son. In those chilly early hours, did Isaac laugh? As the noonday sun loomed over them, did he talk about his plans for the future? As they lay down in the evening to rest, did Abraham weep? With every step, the question repeated—would Abraham hide in God as his shield? In this most devastating test, would he remain faithful?

On the third day of their climb, Abraham spotted the place God had told him to go. "Stay here," he told the servants, and he laid the wood on young Isaac's back. When he clutched the fire and the knife, Isaac realized something was missing. "Father!" he said. "Where is the lamb?"

Abraham touched the shoulder of his son, his only son that he loved. Soon, Isaac must become the sacrifice. But even if his son died on the altar, Abraham trusted that God would not break his promise. God's faithfulness was stronger than death. "God will provide for himself the lamb," he assured Isaac (Genesis 22:7-8).

They reached the place where God led them, and the father built the altar and laid the son on the wood. Abraham's withered hands shook as he stared into his beloved Isaac's eyes as he bound him. As Abraham raised the knife over his only son's heart, did Isaac feel betrayed? Did he look into his father's eyes and cry out, "Why have you forsaken me?"

But after that agonizing moment, relief came. The "angel of the Lord"—that same angel many scholars believe is the Lord Jesus Christ—stopped the father's hand (Genesis 22:11).

Jesus stopped the sacrifice. He knew that someday *he* would walk upon these same mountains, carrying on his back the wooden cross where he would offer himself up, the willing Lamb of God.

The traditional name for the story of the near sacrifice of Isaac is "The Binding of Isaac." When we look at the baby in the manger, we see the God of the universe bound for the first time by his mother as she dressed her helpless infant in swaddling clothes. And there's another time. But that time it was not swaddling clothes, but burial linens that bound him (John 19:40).

Jesus was the Lamb God provided, and just as Isaac was freed from the ropes that bound him, so the baby in the manger would grow up to conquer even stronger bindings, death itself. Death had no hold over Jesus, and Jesus freely, willingly trampled death by dying. But he didn't die for himself, nor did he rise from the grave for his own sake. He was already the Resurrection and the Life! But he was raised from death so he could free us from our own bindings and into the freedom of his life.

Our sins are debts that none can pay but Christ. It is not our tears, but His blood; it is not our sighs, but His sufferings, that can testify for our sins. Christ must pay all, or we are prisoners forever.

THOMAS BROOKS

Because of Jesus's great love and sacrifice, we can love and sacrifice too. What is a real-life way you can show God's radical love to those in your world during this busy season?

REFLECT

Has God ever asked you to do something you really didn't want to do (offer an apology, let go of a grudge, or change your plans to help someone in need)? Right now, is there anything God is asking you to do that you would rather avoid? How can you walk in obedience in that area? (John 15:5; 1 Corinthians 10:13; Psalm 139:23-24)

Lord, I don't know how to adequately thank you for your sacrifice.
Bind my heart to you and let the abundance
of your love splash onto those around me.

Genesis 22

WHO IS THIS SO WEAK AND HELPLESS?
Walsham How (ca. 1867)

Who is this so weak and helpless,
Child of lowly Hebrew maid,
Rudely in a stable sheltered,
Coldly in a manger laid?
'Tis the Lord of all creation,
Who this wondrous path hath trod;
He is God from everlasting,
And to everlasting God.

Who is this, a Man of Sorrows,
Walking sadly life's hard way,

Homeless, weary, sighing, weeping
Over sin and Satan's sway?
'Tis our God, our glorious Savior,
Who above the starry sky
Now for us a place prepareth,
Where no tear can dim the eye.

Who is this? Behold him shedding
Drops of blood upon the ground!
Who is this, despised, rejected,
Mocked, insulted, beaten, bound?
'Tis our God, who gifts and graces
On his church now poureth down;
Who shall smite in holy vengeance
All his foes beneath his throne.

Who is this that hangeth dying
While the rude world scoffs and scorns,
Numbered with the malefactors,
Torn with nails, and crowned with thorns?
'Tis the God who ever liveth
'Mid the shining ones on high,
In the glorious golden city,
Reigning everlastingly.

8

LEAH'S PRAISE

*Why are you cast down, O my soul, and why are
you in turmoil within me? Hope in God; for I shall
again praise him, my salvation and my God.*

PSALM 42:11

I didn't know I would love him.

Leah rubbed her calloused fingers as she sat outside her tent, mending her husband Jacob's tunic. The air seemed still, hot, like a blanket. She glanced back at their bed, at the colorful woolen bedspread she'd made—spun the wool, gathered the herbs for the dye, soaked and wrung the color into the strands. *Would Jacob appreciate her labor?* she had wondered. *Would he care about the blanket?* He had barely noticed it, except to comment on Leah's sister Rachel's fine care of the wool-producing sheep.

More than seven years earlier, Jacob had arrived to the well. His forehead and cheeks were caked in grime, his tunic soiled from sleeping outside. He had traveled eastward, away from his father's land, toward his mother's tribe, to Laban, his uncle, who was Leah's father. Leah's sister Rachel, the shepherdess, had been the first to meet him. She said he looked more like a vagrant than the heir to a great family. But then, like a god, his muscular arms hefted the huge rock from the mouth of the well for her so she could water the sheep. Leah's husband had loved Rachel from that first moment.

Leah shook out the tunic she had mended so expertly. She'd even double-stitched the seam. She didn't want to be the wife of a man who despised her. Her father, Laban, had used the blinding veil of night to trick Jacob into marrying her. Ironic that Jacob had used a similar deception to trick his own father into giving him what should have belonged to his brother. Drunk from the wedding feast, Jacob hadn't realized his new bride wasn't his beloved Rachel, but *her*. Leah, the droopy-eyed girl he didn't want, hadn't chosen. He, the second-born son, had asked for the second-born daughter. But in *this* place, they didn't give the younger before the firstborn. So, he took the woman he didn't love as his wife—but only as the path he had to travel to marry the one who held his heart.

Leah folded the tunic, fresh and ready for him to wear. She imagined his face, his strength, his position. She had given herself to him, and despite his coldness, she loved him. The wind carried the sound of their voices, and Leah knew Jacob and Rachel were strolling back from the fields. She worked alongside him while Leah stayed in the tents.

"Leah," Jacob called as he passed. "Dinner."

As Leah walked to the cooking tent, she prayed to Jacob's God. "Please, Lord, if I have a son, Jacob will know that I am worthy. Do you see me? I who am loved less?" Nine months later, a son arrived—Jacob's firstborn. Holding the strong boy, surely destined for greatness, she named him Rueben, which means "Look, a son!" With this name, she recognized that God had seen her affliction. She prayed that now Jacob would see her.

But no. Bearing a son didn't make him love her. "Another child," she cried out to God. "Please!" She conceived again. "The Lord has heard that I am hated," she said. But her heart's desire to be loved by Jacob still eluded her. Another son came. "Now, this time, my husband will be attached to me, because I have borne him three sons" (Genesis 29:34).

Again, Leah conceived, but Jacob's heart still belonged to Rachel.

Frigid air chilled her face when the first labor pains stirred her from sleep. She knew that in a few hours, her fourth child would arrive in the world. She rolled over, unconcerned about waking her husband, for he did not sleep in her tent. Putting on her cloak, she walked outside.

A delicate sliver of moon lingered above a murky horizon. She watched it disappear, heart twisting as she remembered her husband's absence. But slowly, a far more glorious tapestry wove across the sky. A glorious sunrise, singing with heavenly colors and glowing like a message. Jacob had cast her aside, but she had never been unloved. The baby in her womb kicked, reminding her of her prayers for children. God had answered. Wiping a tear, she realized Someone had always seen her, heard her, and answered her longing cries. And this God—Jacob's God, who had become her God too—was her true husband.

"You, little one," Leah whispered later that evening as she held her newborn son, "I will call Judah, for this time I will praise the Lord."

Judah means "praise." Despite a deep fall into sin, God graciously made him the father of a great tribe—a royal tribe! King David, the author of so many psalms of praise, also came from Judah's line. When the nation split in two, the whole Southern Kingdom was named Judah. And after God's people were exiled for their disobedience, only this tribe returned. All these distinctions single out Judah as a special line, but the tribe of Judah was given an even greater honor.

The Messiah would come from this tribe.

We knew he would come from Judah when Jacob prophesied it on his deathbed (Genesis 49:10). How like God to pick the youngest son of Leah to become the greatest among all the tribes. Someday, Jesus himself would carry on this lineage both literally and spiritually. "He was despised and rejected by men, a man of sorrows and acquainted with grief; and as one from whom men hide their faces he was despised, and we esteemed him not" (Isaiah 53:3). Also, "He came to his own, and his own people did not receive him" (John 1:11). He became an outcast, like Leah, like us.

Come unto me, Jesus might say, all you
who are unloved, unwanted, thrown away
like garbage, for I will treasure you.

CHAD BIRD

We often desire things that don't satisfy. That's because nothing in this world fills the emptiness in our hearts—only God's love has this power. Evaluate your desires in light of God's love. Today, recognize and release your wants and longings for earthly things, and remember that God alone can make you complete.

Remember a time when you desperately desired something only to find when you received it, fulfillment still escaped you. What might this teach you about the unfulfilled longings you have today?
(John 4:13-15; Romans 12:2)

PRAY

Jesus, lover of my soul, help me value your love above all other loves.

READ

Genesis 29

SING

O COME, O COME, EMMANUEL

Latin antiphons (12th century), Latin hymn (1710),
translated by John Mason Neale (1851)

O come, O come, Emmanuel,
And ransom captive Israel,
That mourns in lonely exile here,
Until the Son of God appear.

Refrain:
Rejoice! Rejoice! Emmanuel
Shall come to thee, O Israel.

O come, O come, thou Lord of might,
Who to thy tribes, on Sinai's height,
In ancient times didst give the law
In cloud and majesty and awe. [Refrain]

O come, thou Rod of Jesse, free
Thine own from Satan's tyranny;
From depths of hell thy people save,
And give them victory o'er the grave. [Refrain]

O come, thou Dayspring from on high
And cheer us by thy drawing nigh;
Disperse the gloomy clouds of night,
And death's dark shadows put to flight. [Refrain]

O come, thou Key of David, come
And open wide our heav'nly home;
Make safe the way that leads on high,
And close the path to misery. [Refrain]

9

JUDAH'S FEAR

Peace I leave with you; my peace I give to you. Not
as the world gives do I give to you. Let not your
hearts be troubled, neither let them be afraid.

JOHN 14:27

A father sends out his robe-wearing son, who encounters murderous men—his own brothers—waiting for him. He is thrown into a pit and then descends into a far-away land. Many believe him to be dead. Yet, he rises again to the right hand of the king and saves the world by bringing life-giving bread to the starving. Whose story is this? Joseph's! (Genesis 37–50).

It's hard not to see Jesus in the details of Joseph's epic story—sent by a father, descends to a hellish pit, rises again to the right hand of the high king. And yet, alongside Joseph's faithful suffering and exaltation, we find a contrasting story that is equally as epic—the story of rugged and ragged men, broken by their own disloyalty, jealousy, and shame.

At the end of another day with no rain, Jacob gazed at his hungry and parched grandchildren, who were growing weaker in the desolate land. Jacob's soul ached. When the famine hit, he had watched his large family's food supply dwindle. He had eleven sons, one daughter, their spouses, plus many grandchildren to feed. As the hot breeze blew over him, Jacob pondered the promise made to his grandfather Abraham, declaring that their line would be a blessing to many nations (Genesis 12:1-3). But if they died from starvation, how would that happen?

One day, a traveler came through, informing him that grain was available to buy in Egypt. In Jacob's desperate need, God had provided. Sitting in the door of his tent, he gathered his sons to him. "Go down," he said, "and buy grain for us there, that we may live and not die" (Genesis 42:2).

He sent all except Benjamin, his new favorite son. He already lost his beloved Joseph. He couldn't bear to lose Benjamin too. Watching his sons disappear over the horizon, his heart ached. "O God, guide their footsteps. Lead them to peace."

Judah[1] was not the firstborn. He was Leah's fourth child, but somehow, he had become the leader among his brothers. Thankful to be able to help provide for his family, he led the others on the long, rugged journey down to Egypt.

Finally arriving, they immediately went to the man who was doling out the grain, "This line is never-ending," Asher said as they waited.

Judah wiped the sweat from his brow. "But thanks be to God that we are here. This time tomorrow we will be heading home with food for our children."

"What he means is, stop complaining." Rueben peered at Asher who lowered his eyes.

Judah examined the busy city, clearly not crippled by the famine. So many people, houses, roads, horses—very different from his nomadic life. And the aromas! A mix of cooking meat, spices he didn't recognize, and all kinds of not-so-pleasant scents as well. This was not the place for him. He would be glad to get home.

When their turn finally came, Judah, along with his brothers, bowed to the ground before the king's ruler. The man looked them over, as if inspecting each one. Finally, he said, "You are spies!"

Judah's heart sank. *What? Why would he think that?* "We, your servants, are twelve brothers, the sons of one man in the land of Canaan, and behold, the youngest is this day with our father, and one is no more" (Genesis 42:13).

Still, the ruler insisted they were spies.

Panic grew in Judah's chest. Surely, they'd be denied the grain they so desperately needed. Would they also be imprisoned? Killed? The very afflictions they had connived for Joseph now threatened them.

Finally the ruler agreed to let them go with more bags of grain than they'd asked for, but with one stipulation.

"Bring your youngest brother to me."

Benjamin? No. Why? Judah knew their father would never allow it. He'd be devastated were they even to ask. Judah and his brothers trembled in fear.

As the ruler's servants loaded their donkeys with the grain sacks, the guilt he had stifled for years rose to the surface. "It's because of what we did to Joseph," he said. "God is repaying us!"

As they headed home, Judah rode silently. The air seemed still. Crows circled, interested in the grain bags. The mood among his brothers was as bleak as the terrain.

And then it got worse. When they stopped to feed their donkeys, they found the money they had paid for the grain hiding in their sacks. Again, fear struck them. They were being framed for stealing. But what could they do? They continued their journey home.

When they arrived, Jacob refused to allow them to return with Benjamin. Months passed. The famine worsened. Finally, when they had swallowed their last bite of bread, Judah went to his father. He offered himself as a pledge. If Benjamin didn't return, he himself would carry the blame. And so, with weak confidence in Judah, Jacob allowed Benjamin to go with the others.

When they once again reached Egypt, Judah and his brothers were immediately escorted to see Joseph—at his house. And again they were terrified.

With every event that happened, fear, panic, trembling, and even tearing clothes continued. Grisly fear that at any moment the truth of their treacherous treatment of their brother would be exposed.

And then it was. This powerful Egyptian stranger revealed that he was neither an Egyptian nor a stranger. He was Joseph! The one they had betrayed. The one they never expected to see again. Judah dared to gaze into the eyes of this man, his brother! Joseph had every right to condemn them to death for their crimes, but far from a judging, condemning glare, tender love brought Joseph to tears. Then he surprised them again, demonstrating not only mercy but generosity. Joseph gave them the best land in Egypt, an abundance of food, and supplies for the family to travel.

They gathered their father, Jacob, and their families, and then lived in Egypt for many years, safe in their brother's care.

But after Jacob died, they again fell into the pit of fear. Judah and his brothers approached Joseph. Would he finally repay them for the evil they had done to him? Joseph smiled. No. Instead, he spoke life-giving words. "'You meant evil against me, but God meant it for good…So do not fear; I will provide for you and your little ones.' Thus he comforted them and spoke kindly to them" (Genesis 50:20-21). After all the examples of Judah and his brothers' fearfulness, how apt that this story—and the whole book of Genesis—conclude with this sentiment: *Do not fear.*

Joseph's love draws from God's abundant reservoir of love. The words, *do not fear* run like a gentle stream through the redemption story, even finding their way to a field on the outskirts of a certain little town: "In the same region there were shepherds out in the field, keeping watch over their flock by night. And an angel of the Lord appeared to them, and the glory of the Lord shone around them, and they were filled with great fear. And the angel said to them, 'Do not fear, for behold, I bring you good news of great joy that will be for all the people'" (Luke 2:8-10).

When confronted with the holiness of God, our first response is to tremble. We know God has every right to judge us, and we know we'd be found guilty. But the truth is that the one who holds the power of life and death, the very one against whom we have sinned, forgives us! Freely, generously, willingly. So, listen to what he says over and over again: *Do not fear!*

If the Lord be with us, we have no cause of fear. His eye is upon us, His arm over us, His ear open to our prayer—His grace sufficient, His promise unchangeable.

JOHN NEWTON

PRACTICE

Like Joseph's brothers, we are often fearful, as if Jesus might somehow leave us, or judge us, or stop loving us. His Word is greater than our fears: "Thus says the LORD, he who created you, O Jacob, he who formed you, O Israel: 'Fear not, for I have redeemed you; I have called you by name, you are mine'" (Isaiah 43:1).

Return to this promise the next time you feel afraid.

Describe a time when you acted out of fear instead of faith.
How often do you do this? How can you walk in the truth that
you are loved (Romans 8:15)?

*Father, I confess that like Joseph's brothers, I doubt your love and cling
to fear far too much. Help me rest in your love, always.*

Genesis 37–50

WHILE SHEPHERDS WATCHED THEIR FLOCKS
Nahum Tate (1700)

While shepherds watched their flocks by night,
All seated on the ground,
The angel of the Lord came down,
And glory shone around.

"Fear not," said he—for mighty dread
Had seized their troubled mind—

"Glad tidings of great joy I bring
To you and all mankind.

"To you in David's town this day,
Is born of David's line,
The Savior, who is Christ, the Lord,
And this shall be the sign.

"The heav'nly Babe you there shall find
To human view displayed,
All meanly wrapped in swathing bands,
And in a manger laid."

10

JOCHEBED'S ARK

*The Lord is faithful. He will establish you
and guard you from the evil one.*

2 THESSALONIANS 3:3

I will keep him safe.

Smoky scents from morning fires wafted to Jochebed as she woke in her
cot from a restless sleep. Head pounding, back aching, she sat up and drew
her groggy newborn to her. As the eager infant latched on, anxiety seized her,
as it did every morning.

Her two lively older children, Aaron and Miriam, bounded into her room,
full of stories about the other's naughty antics. She managed a weak smile
before sending them out to press olives for oil.

A little later, after dressing and weaving her hair into a tight bun, she fixed
her newborn into his sling against her chest, and sat down at their table for a
meager breakfast. As their fingers shoved the cakes first into the oil, and then
into their mouths, she tried to navigate their barrage of questions.

"No, father is already working. He will be home when the taskmaster says.
Aaron, you know this."

"Miriam, please don't tease the baby. Now he's crying—"

Soldiers' footsteps pounded down the road, and Jochebed grasped the tiny babe more tightly to her chest, rushing to the back room. "Hush, little one. Hush."

If a soldier heard her child's cries, if he was reported, then this dear one…she couldn't bear the possibility. Never again would her arms hold him. Never again would she smell his sweet hair. Never again would she feel him next to her. Into the Nile he would disappear forever, an offering to Anubis, the Egyptian god of death. The soldiers' footsteps faded, but still her mind wandered toward Pharaoh's heartless command. *Why?* her heart cried. Jochebed meant "Yahweh glorified." She wanted to glorify the God of her people, but how could he bring glory out of this?

She gazed at her newborn, now smiling, and contemplated him. Those eyes—so like his father's! The strong grip of his fingers on hers, and oh how he ate! Yet, Jochebed saw something more than excellent physical characteristics in this child. He was a "good"[1] child. "Good, like your creation," she whispered to God. "Good like you." When she gazed in curious wonder over her son, Jochebed somehow saw that he would find favor in God's sight, that God's presence would go with him. No matter what Pharaoh ordered, she would not hand him over to the Egyptians to die. She would continue to hide him.

Three months later, after a day of desperately attempting to quiet her baby's cries, she sat in her doorway, praying. "Please, God, bless and keep this child. Spare his life. Show me what to do." The sound of heavy footsteps again approached, and her heart clenched, but it was only her husband, home from another day laboring under their harsh masters. Eyeing his hands, calloused from forming bricks out of straw and mud, an idea whispered to her mind.

She could weave a basket. She remembered the pitch Noah the ark builder used to seal his floating haven. She could cover her basket with pitch too. Yes, her hands would craft a refuge for her son, his own little ark. She wove a papyrus basket for him, covered it with pitch, and then she carefully placed the child within his new crib. With shaking hands, she set it among the reeds along the bank of the Nile.

Unlike when she defied Pharoah by hiding the baby, this time she would obey the letter of the law. "You want me to throw my boy into the Nile? Very well, Pharaoh. You didn't say I couldn't put him in a waterproof basket first."

Yet, this journey was far from safe. Strong waves. Rapids. Crocodiles, venomous snakes, hippopotami threatened her child's safety. Sister Miriam followed and watched.

But no wave drowned Moses. No crocodile ate him. Instead, God gently guided the little ark. The vulnerable baby traveled safely through the waters, arriving exactly where God planned so that one day he would grow up to deliver God's people from the vicious bonds of murderous pharaoh. And he would guide them through another dangerous river, that time on dry land.

In the fullness of time, another "good" son was born into life-threatening conditions. The infant-king broke into this world, vulnerable in the womb of a virgin whose tender youth could have been unjustly snuffed out for adultery. Miscarriage certainly loomed as they bumped along the treacherous journey to Bethlehem on a donkey. It's a wonder this deliverer ever arrived in Bethlehem to be born.

Like Moses, Jesus was born under the threat of an evil king's murderous command to destroy infants. But despite the dangers, in a tiny stable on a chilly dawn, young Mary held an even greater deliverer than Moses in her arms. Their small family escaped *to* Egypt this time (instead of *from* Egypt).

Both Moses's and Jesus's dangerous journeys were governed by God's hand of providence. No danger could thwart God's purpose. And no matter the heartache or stress or obstacles that come our way, nothing can hinder his loving purpose for us.

*Through many dangers toils and snares I have
already come. 'Tis grace that brought me safe
thus far, and grace will lead me home.*

JOHN NEWTON

We've each faced dangers and sorrows. Perhaps you remember the
coldness of a dying parent's hand, or the disappointment of an
unwanted negative pregnancy test. Sometimes the path to God's
love is laden with peril. But today, remember that he is good.
He is the river of life.

When has God led you safely through danger? How can
you draw on memories of his past provision to find new courage
in him today? (Psalm 23:4; 34:6)

*Thank you, sovereign God, that you don't allow anything to block
my path that could keep you from directing my ways. When physical,
emotional, or spiritual dangers encircle me, draw me into your
protection. Comfort me with the knowledge of your all-powerful
and eternally loving care.*

READ

Exodus 1–2

SING

GO TELL IT ON THE MOUNTAIN

African American spiritual, stanzas John W. Work III (1907)

Refrain:
Go tell it on the mountain,
Over the hills, and ev'rywhere;
Go, tell it on the mountain
That Jesus Christ is born.

While shepherds kept their watching
O'er silent flocks by night,
Behold, throughout the heavens
There shone a holy light. [Refrain]

The shepherds feared and trembled
When lo, above the earth
Rang out the angel chorus
That hailed our Savior's birth. [Refrain]

Down in a lowly manger
the humble Christ was born,
And God sent us salvation
That blessed Christmas morn. [Refrain]

11

ISRAEL'S BREAD

Jesus said to them, "I am the bread of life; whoever comes to me shall not hunger, and whoever believes in me shall never thirst."

JOHN 6:35

After the Red Sea's parting, the Israelites' hearts had erupted in shouts of worship to the God who pressed the sea into sky-scraping walls of water, allowing their sandals, unmuddied, to stride safely through a sea-test they should not have survived. They sang, "The LORD is my strength and my song!" (Exodus 15:2).

But after this victorious moment, a long journey into a hot wilderness awaited them. For two and a half months, they slogged along, their jubilant choruses drying in their mouths like desert sand.

And their stomachs were the first to revolt. Would God provide food for them in the desolate wasteland? Surely not. How could he? Their weakened animals faltered, their little ones whined for home, and soon the whole congregation, moving as one, confronted Moses and Aaron, frenzied, terrified, accusatory. "If only we had died by the LORD's hand in Egypt!" (Exodus 16:3 NIV). Like the Egyptian's firstborn during Passover? Is that what they were asking for?

They voiced their complaint to the God who had crushed Ra and Isis and Heqet beneath plagues of darkness and hail and frogs. They accused the God who saved them, who claimed them as his own, who led in "steadfast love" (Exodus 15:13). Steadfast love! That miraculous word (*hesed* in Hebrew), which mystifies translation but reaches deeper than Jacob's well to the depth of longing. Father love. Covenant love. Knowing love. Forgiving love. Everlasting love.[1]

And yet, the people for whom God had already accomplished the impossible could not see a way of survival. There was no food. No water. "We're tired. It's sand and more sand. We can't live here. We want to go back to Egypt."

Out of his patient love, God provided for the anxious Israelites during their journey. As they lobbed their doubts upward, fragile flakes fluttered down, bread of heaven, tasting sweet, like the promised land, that land of milk and honey. "He rained down on them manna to eat and gave them the grain of heaven. Man ate of the bread of the angels; he sent them food in abundance" (Psalm 78:24-25).

In a way, God sent manna to Joseph and Mary too. The true Bread of Heaven rested in Mary's arms. The bread in the desert pointed to him. The more-than bread. The life-giver who provides not just food, but everything!

Jesus is the true manna, the real provision (John 6:31-35). Feeding on God's heavenly manna satisfies our hearts' otherwise insatiable hunger. When he says to us, "Take, eat," we open our mouths and finally, after all our earthly travels, we taste and are satisfied. And having tasted of Christ, we can then join Mary in saying, "My soul magnifies the Lord…He has filled the hungry with good things" (Luke 1:46, 53).

*Jesus did not come into the world mainly
to give bread, but to be bread.*

JOHN PIPER

When God's provision didn't appear, the Israelites panicked, but Joseph and Mary acted in trust. The cure for moments of desperate panic is partaking of the Bread of Heaven by reading the Word, journaling, prayer, worship. Go to him and receive your fill— as much as you can "eat"! This bread will never run out.

Can you think of a time when God provided for you? Have you ever doubted that he would supply your needs? Describe your experience. (Matthew 6:34; Psalm 23:1)

O Father, too many times I complain, I panic, I fear. Yet, out of your steadfast love, even when my faith faints like a food-deprived Israelite, you still provide. Your provision isn't always easy to see, so please help me, even when it's hidden from me, to rest in your care.

READ

Exodus 16

SING

IT CAME UPON A MIDNIGHT CLEAR
Edmund H. Sears (1849)

It came upon the midnight clear,
That glorious song of old,
From angels bending near the earth
To touch their harps of gold:
"Peace on the earth, good will to men,
From heaven's all-gracious King:"
The world in solemn stillness lay,
To hear the angels sing.

Still through the cloven skies they come,
With peaceful wings unfurled,
And still their heav'nly music floats
O'er all the weary world:
Above its sad and lowly plains
They bend on hov'ring wing,
And ever o'er its Babel sounds
The blessed angels sing.

And ye, beneath life's crushing load,
Whose forms are bending low,
Who toil along the climbing way

With painful steps and slow,
Look now! for glad and golden hours
Come swiftly on the wing:
O rest beside the weary road,
And hear the angels sing.

For lo, the days are hastening on,
By prophet bards foretold,
When with the ever-circling years
Comes round the age of gold;
When peace shall over all the earth
Its ancient splendors fling,
And the whole world give back the song
Which now the angels sing.

12

JOSHUA'S TRUST

I am the LORD; I have called you in righteousness;
I will take you by the hand and keep you.

ISAIAH 42:6

Joshua walked through the empty wilderness, away from the chaos
of camp. He needed to be alone. His time of mourning the loss of Moses was
over, but he still missed his beloved mentor. How would he ever be a leader
like the one who had walked with God's rebellious, chosen people through
ten plagues in Egypt, a sea parting, and forty hungry-thirsty years wandering the desert? He had been prophet, priest, and king to those he nurtured
as his own—saving, watching, keeping, loving a whole nation. Joshua drew
in a breath of the desert air, and paused at a lone acacia tree to rest and ponder his beloved mentor, who was more like a father to him.

Had any leader ever poured out his life more sacrificially than Moses? Joshua
thought of the many young children he'd blessed who now stood as men and
women. All their parents, save for two undaunted warriors, were dead. This
new generation of never-been-slaves now had to restart the task of conquering the promised land that their forefathers had been too frightened to complete—these ones raised in Moses's care, touched by his wrinkled hands, led

by his calloused feet. But could they win the battles their parents had lost? Would they trust Moses's admonition to cling to the only one who saved?

A wind stirred up, and Joshua resumed walking, edging closer to the Jordan River. When they first arrived at the edge of this waterway, so many years ago, Moses knew only the Lord's power could deliver the land into Israel's hands. Joshua's birth name was Hoshea, which meant "Save!" In a subtle hint, Moses changed Joshua's name to *the Lord saves* (Numbers 13:16). Joshua had to cling to God for strength. There was no other way to win the battles that waited. In a sense, Moses was telling the beloved young man, "Remember, don't let go of God's hand."

Later, God reiterated this message himself. "As I was with Moses, so I will be with you; I will never leave you nor forsake you...Do not be frightened and do not be dismayed" (Joshua 1:5, 9).

At first, Joshua embraced this promise. As the winds of battle with Jericho grew closer, Joshua's battle-worn hand gripped his Father's like a child unsure of his first steps, constantly peering to him for guidance, praying, "Do you want me to take this great city?" And God faithfully answered him. Seven times in the first six chapters of the book of Joshua, we read, "The LORD said to Joshua." Mighty Captain Joshua's successes came not from himself but from relying on the true Commander of the Lord's armies.

And when the time came, Joshua immediately obeyed God's strange instructions (Joshua 6:1-7). The Israelites marched. They shouted. The great city of Jericho fell in an amazing victory!

But after this miraculous triumph, something changed. The next city they approached was called Ai, which means "the heap." Not an enticing place. Nothing like mighty Jericho, Ai was a small city. Joshua sent only a few troops.

But they lost. Many Israelites died.

We lost? Joshua was crushed. "Then Joshua tore his clothes and fell to the earth on his face before the ark of the LORD until the evening, he and the elders of Israel. And they put dust on their heads. And Joshua said, 'Alas, O Lord GOD, why have you brought this people over the Jordan at all, to give us into the hands of the Amorites, to destroy us? Would that we had been content to dwell beyond the Jordan!'" (Joshua 7:6-7).

God graciously exposed the reason they lost. A man named Achan—whose name derived from the word for trouble—had stolen a cloak, silver, and gold from Jericho and buried these spoils of war under his tent. After God punished Achan, with God's guidance, Joshua led his warriors to again engage in battle with Ai. This time they won.

The next morning, perhaps Joshua again searched for solitude. *Why did God not reveal Achan's sin before the battle of Ai?* He knew the answer. Joshua hadn't been listening. He was gaining fame and with it, pride. After faithfully seeking the Lord's guidance with the battle of Jericho, when he saw that Ai was a smaller, easily defeated enemy, like a child, he let go of his Father's hand, ran ahead without seeking the Lord.

Another warrior named "God will save" (Jesus is the Greek name for Joshua) also wrapped his hand—tiny, creased, new—around the hands of the parents who cared for him. The infant conqueror, wet and cold, donned humanity's fragile coat, dependent on others to tend his needs, just as throughout his life he maintained his childlike dependence on his heavenly Father (John 8:29). He perfectly listened, relied upon, and obeyed God every day of his life, prepared to face a battle greater than Ai or Jericho—the battle for our souls against darkness, sin, and Satan himself. Jesus fought to the death, and by his death, he conquered. He bore our sins and bestowed life onto those of us who, like Joshua, sometimes let go of our Father's hand (1 Peter 2:24; Romans 5:8; Ephesians 2:4-6).

Alone with none but thee, my God,
I journey on my way.
What need I fear, when thou art near O king of night and day?
More safe am I within thy hand
Than if a host did round me stand.

SAINT COLUMBA

Ponder the infant in the manger, and let his fragile state remind you of your own desperate need. Throw your arms around the Lord with abandon. He will not leave you or forsake you. (Deuteronomy 31:6)

Which struggles tempt you to believe you can take care of them on your own? Which anxieties might you feel are too small to be worthy of God's time? What are two or three simple steps you can take to bring your battles to the Lord and remember that he is fighting for you? (1 Peter 5:7; Isaiah 41:13; 2 Chronicles 20:15)

Father God, like Joshua, I often let go of your hand, choosing to trust myself instead. Humble my pride, and may I lose every battle in which I rest in my own strength.

Joshua 6-8

GOD REST YE MERRY, GENTLEMEN

English Carol (18th Century)

God rest you merry, gentlemen,
Let nothing you dismay,
Remember Christ our Savior
Was born on Christmas day,
To save us all from Satan's power
When we were gone astray;

Refrain:
O tidings of comfort and joy, comfort and joy,
O tidings of comfort and joy, comfort and joy.

From God our heav'nly Father,
A blessed angel came;
And unto certain shepherds
Brought tidings of the same:
How that in Bethlehem was born
The son of God by name. [Refrain]

"Fear not then," said the angel,
"Let nothing you affright,

This day is born a Savior
Of a pure virgin bright,
To free all those who trust in him
From Satan's power and might." [Refrain]

The shepherds at those tidings
Rejoiced much in mind,
And left their flocks afeeding,
In tempest, storm, and wind:
And went to Bethlehem straightway,
The Son of God to find. [Refrain]

13

MANOAH'S WONDER

And his name shall be called Wonderful Counselor.

ISAIAH 9:6

There was a certain man of Zorah, of the tribe of the Danites, whose name was Manoah. And his wife was barren and had no children" (Judges 13:2).

The autumn sun slanted soft shards of light over his hillside orchards as Manoah poured water from a clay pot into the trough for his modest herd of goats. Glancing back at his home, he recalled watching his father place each white stone in its place.

Manoah wished he could provide a place of rest for a family of his own, but the Lord had closed his wife's womb.

A breeze rustled through the oak groves, and he paused in the shade, thanking the Lord for the cool relief from the late-spring heat. He plucked a leaf from a tree and gazed beyond the groves to the field, its breeze-blown barley, still green, cascading down the hill. He was a simple farmer from an unimpressive tribe. He remembered Moses's blessing. "Dan is a lion's cub, springing out of Bashan" (Deuteronomy 33:22 NIV). But in the last few years, his tribe had been routed by the Philistines, and their land had been split into two parts to pacify them. Similar to Moses's, the blessing Jacob had given his son Dan stated that his tribe would look for the deliverance of the Lord

(Genesis 49:18 NIV). Manoah lifted his eyes. Cloud clusters, downy white, were mounded like a citadel against the deep blue sky. He didn't hope for a great deliverance but simply to dwell peacefully on this hill in the shadow of the Almighty.

A goat bleated nearby, and Manoah strolled to it. "You." Manoah patted its creamy tuft of fur. "You are fine and fat. We will save you for a special dinner." It skipped way, as if escaping its fate.

"Manoah!" his wife's voice, breathless, resounded from across the field.

"What is it?" Manoah called. "Did a goat get stuck in a bramble again? Did a messenger come with news of a raid?"

His wife's black braid whipped behind her as she ran. Reaching him, she leaned against the tree, grasping her stomach. As she caught her breath, she managed to tell him about a visitor who had entered the field. "A man of God came to me," she said, "and his appearance was like the appearance of the angel of God, very awesome. I did not ask him where he was from, and he did not tell me his name" (Judges 13:6).

"A man of God? In our field?"

"Yes." She tucked a stray hair behind her ear. "He said to me, 'Behold, you shall conceive and bear a son.'" Her gaze stayed with his as she waited for a response. After a moment, she continued. "He also said, 'So then drink no wine or strong drink, and eat nothing unclean'" (Judges 13:7).

Manoah recognized the Nazarite vow, this lifestyle covenant kept by men consecrated for God who were commanded to not cut their hair, drink wine, or touch anything that would make them impure (Numbers 6:1-8). "Why the Nazarite vow?"

"I don't know—"

Manoah's mind flew in every direction but landed back on the unbelievable news. "We're going to have a baby?" He grabbed her hands. "After all this time? Can it be true?" A laugh escaped. "If a man of God said it, it must be!"

The woman took a breath. "And Manoah, the man said our son will begin to deliver Israel" (Judges 13:6).

After his wife returned to the house, Manoah pondered her words. Was what she said true? And why did the man of God tell the woman and not him? His son would be a deliverer? As the sun sloped behind the horizon, he prayed, "O Lord, please let the man of God whom you sent come again to us and teach us what we are to do with the child who will be born" (Judges 13:8).

God kindly listened to the voice of Manoah. The man who had visited Manoah's wife returned, meeting the two of them in the field among the green barley shafts.

"Are you the man who spoke to this woman?"

And he said, "I am" (Judges 13:11).

"Let us feed you one of our goats," Manoah offered, echoing an invitation his forefather Abraham had made to a trio of divine visitors generations earlier.

"No, I will not eat," the visitor said. "But if you want, go ahead and prepare a burnt offering." Perhaps he smiled.

They led the man of God to a rock, a place to make an offering. "What is your name?" Manoah asked him. He recalled how long ago, during his own divine encounter, Manoah's ancestor Jacob had also asked this.

"Why do you ask my name?" The man answered Manoah's question with his own. "It's too full of wonder[1] for you to understand" (Judges 13:18).

Manoah paused. *Full of wonder? How can a name be full of wonder?* He threw his wife a glance. *Who is this man?*

Manoah and his wife laid the grain on the rock, as well as the young goat they had first offered to their visitor, and then they lit the fire for their offering. Manoah's face warmed as the flames began to consume their sacrifice, the rich aroma filling the air. Then, while they watched, something unbelievable happened. "The angel of the LORD went up in the flame of the altar" (Judges 13:20). Immediately, Manoah and his wife fell on their faces to the ground.

The man had been the angel of the Lord—that same angel we've already encountered, the very Son of God, walking on earth before he became flesh. It was him all along. As with Moses's bush and Abraham's firepot, he was there, dangerous and compassionate and radiant in the flames.

Manoah was blind to the presence of God. Yet, with great patience, the Lord announced the birth of the mighty judge Samson who would "begin to save Israel from the hand of the Philistines" (Judges 13:5). But when he learned whose presence he was really in—the presence of the Holy One, Jesus (though he didn't know his name), wonder threw him and his wife to the ground in worship.

Centuries later, another father, Joseph, was not the first to be told. He too didn't know the Son of God was dwelling close by. He too was a man who trusted the Lord. And his son would not just deliver Israel from her earthly oppressors, but become Israel's ultimate deliverer (Matthew 1:18-25).

And we, too, can fall at his feet in awe of who he is.

O come, O come, and be our God-with-us
O long-sought With-ness for a world without,
O secret seed, O hidden spring of light.
Come to us Wisdom, come unspoken Name
Come Root, and Key, and King, and holy Flame.

MALCOLM GUITE

PRACTICE

The presence of the man of God whose name was too full of wonder for him to comprehend inspired Manoah to worship. We know his name, the name above all names (Philippians 2:9), Jesus. Reflect on his wonderful name and worship him in your words, thoughts, and actions today and every day.

REFLECT

When do you feel closest to God? When do you feel far from God? What about him inspires wonder in you? (Deuteronomy 31:6; Psalm 139:7-12; 34:18)

PRAY

O Emmanuel, even as Manoah's eyes did not see you,
so my eyes often fail to perceive your presence burning close and strong.
Deliver me from my blindness and help me to live in the shadow
of your holiness, protected by your love.

READ

Judges 13

SING

THE SANDS OF TIME ARE SINKING
(In Emmanuel's Land)

Anne R. Cousin (1857) based on letters of Samuel Rutherford (1600–1661)

The sands of time are sinking,
The dawn of heaven breaks,
The summer morn I've sighed for,
The fair sweet morn awakes;
Dark, dark, hath been the midnight,
But dayspring is at hand,
And glory, glory dwelleth
In Emmanuel's land.

The King there in his beauty
Without a veil is seen;
It were a well-spent journey
Though seven deaths lay between:
The Lamb with his fair army
Doth on Mount Zion stand,
And glory, glory dwelleth
In Emmanuel's land.

O Christ, he is the fountain,
The deep sweet well of love!
The streams on earth I've tasted

More deep I'll drink above:
There to an ocean fullness
His mercy doth expand,
And glory, glory dwelleth
In Emmanuel's land.

The bride eyes not her garment,
But her dear bridegroom's face;
I will not gaze at glory,
But on my King of grace;
Not at the crown he gifteth,
But on his pierced hand:
The Lamb is all the glory
Of Emmanuel's land.

14

NAOMI'S SON

You have turned for me my mourning into dancing; you have loosed my sackcloth; and clothed me with gladness.

PSALM 30:11

Famine had seared the little town of Bethlehem. The city of bread had no bread, so Naomi's husband Elimelech, whose name meant "my God is king," led their family east, taking his wife and his sons Mahlon and Chilion away from their God's kingdom to live among idol worshipers in Moab.

Although leaving home had wounded her heart, at least Naomi had her beloved husband and sons, two fine heirs who were the hope of her heart. Their presence was a promise that she'd be secure in her old age, surrounded by loved ones to care for her even though they dwelled in a country so far away from the land of promise.

But one day, as chants from the Moabites' worship feasts echoed through the hills, Elimelech died. O, the pain that wracked Naomi's heart. What comfort did she have? Thankfully, her two sons remained. She showered them with love, her heart rejoicing with hope that they would soon give her grandchildren.

But tragedy shattered her again when her two boys suddenly died.

How great Naomi's loss—one husband, two heirs, all certainty of a stable future.

I'm completely alone, she thought. As days passed, though her daughters-in-law promised to care for her, Naomi refused any comfort from them. These widows were still young. They needed to move on to their new lives. Angry tears continued to dampen Naomi's blankets as torrents of bitter thoughts spun, agonizing her heart. How could God take her loved ones from her? She had become as a barren woman with no one left to carry on her husband's name. And without family to care for her, she would starve. She was alone, abandoned by God—as good as dead.

After another night of mourning, Naomi lumbered out of bed. The sun crept from behind Mount Nebo, and she gazed at the hills, the neighbors' homes, the dusty road that led to the marketplace. This foreign land that had become home suddenly looked abhorrent to her. "I will not stay in this cursed land," she decided. She may as well perish in her own homeland.

Once she had packed, she gave her home a final glance—*there, that's where little Mahlon fell and got the scar on his forehead. And there, baby Chilion and I used to cuddle early before anyone woke up. That old wooden table, how many meals did I share there with Elimelech? I can still hear his voice echoing through the room.*

Without looking back, she began to walk westward toward Bethlehem, the land of her birth and the land of the God who failed her. It would be a long and dangerous journey for an old woman traveling alone. *But what does my life even matter?*

But as she started out, her daughters-in-law joined her. Why would they come? She couldn't fathom. She was too old to have any hope of more sons for them to marry. What future could she offer them? "Go, return each of you to her mother's house," she told them. "May the LORD deal kindly with you, as you have dealt with the dead and with me" (Ruth 1:8). She pleaded with them to go back to their own families, their own gods.

Tearfully, daughter-in-law Orpah finally obeyed, kissing Naomi goodbye—but Ruth didn't. "Ruth said, 'Do not urge me to leave you or to return from following you. For where you go I will go, and where you lodge I will lodge. Your people shall be my people, and your God my God'" (Ruth 1:16). And so together they set out for Bethlehem.

When they arrived, the townspeople recognized Naomi. Time had passed, but Naomi's grief still wracked her heart. "Do not call me Naomi; call me Mara [bitter]," she said, "for the Almighty has dealt very bitterly with me" (Ruth 1:20). Lost in her own sorrow, she fled from her only comfort.

Undeterred by her rebellion, God saw Naomi in her sorrow. He would not cast her aside like the stray grains the harvesters left behind in the fields that Naomi's daughter-in-law Ruth gathered to place upon their table. God used even these scraps for his glory. Ruth "just so happened" to glean barley in a field that belonged to Naomi's kinsman, Boaz. Boaz, who could marry Ruth, and who could redeem Naomi's fractured bloodline.[1] This man noticed Ruth's persistent labor. He admired her courage in venturing to Bethlehem and her tenderness toward her mother-in-law. Boaz flooded her bags with food. He protected Ruth. And soon, he loved her—so much that he made her his wife, redeeming both Ruth and Naomi from their lowly status as widows without heirs.

But even more blessings graced Naomi, for not only had her security been repaired by the marriage of Ruth to Boaz, but when the couple had a child, in the eyes of their culture, Naomi's womb was also made new. "And the women of the neighborhood gave him a name, saying, 'A son has been born to Naomi'" (Ruth 4:17). To Naomi? Yes, the child was called hers. So…a baby born in Bethlehem brought new life to a broken woman. But who was this incredible child? "They named him Obed. He was the father of Jesse, the father of David" (Ruth 4:17).

Through this bitter woman and her outcast daughter-in-law would come two great kings! The first would be King David, ancient Israel's most faithful king, a ruler who was called "a man after [God's] own heart" (1 Samuel 13:14). And from David would come another King, one even greater than him. This most high King who would come through Naomi's line—and who was hinted at by Boaz's redemption of Naomi and Ruth—was Jesus.

I have reason to praise him for my trials, for, most probably, I should have been ruined without them.

JOHN NEWTON

PRACTICE

We don't understand why heartbreak must enter our lives, and when it does, trust can dry up like fields in a famine. Remember how gently God restored Naomi, and take heart, confident that his lovingkindness never fails.

REFLECT

How has God surprised you with his love at a time when you least expected it? What has this taught you about his character and his trustworthiness? (Psalm 36:5-6; 1 John 3:1; Romans 8:38-39)

PRAY

Father of my soul, keep my heart from bitterness.
Help me trust your love.

READ

Ruth

ONCE IN ROYAL DAVID'S CITY

Cecil Frances Alexander (1848)

Once in royal David's city
Stood a lowly cattle shed,
Where a mother laid her baby
In a manger for his bed:
Mary was that mother mild,
Jesus Christ her little child.

He came down to earth from heaven
Who is God and Lord of all,
And his shelter was a stable,
And his cradle was a stall:
With the poor, and mean, and lowly,
Lived on earth our Savior holy.

And, through all his wondrous childhood
He would honor and obey,
Love and watch the lowly maiden
In whose gentle arms he lay:
Christian children all must be
Mild, obedient, good as he.

And our eyes at last shall see him,
Through his own redeeming love;

For that Child so dear and gentle
Is our Lord in heav'n above,
And he leads his children on
To the place where he is gone.

Not in that poor lowly stable,
With the oxen standing by,
We shall see him, but in heaven,
Set at God's right hand on high;
When like stars his children crowned
All in white shall wait around.

15

HANNAH'S JOY

Behold, when the sound of your greeting came to my ears,
the baby in my womb leaped for joy.

LUKE 1:44-45

The tabernacle—that place where the ark of the covenant was kept, where pilgrims came from all over Israel to worship their God—was situated in the hill country of Shiloh when Hannah paid her visits. Every year, Hannah traveled there along with her husband, Elkanah, their servants, and the family's many children. The children only made the journey more difficult, for Hannah was not their mother; rather, they were the offspring of Peninnah, Elkanah's other wife.

Peninnah used these pilgrimages to provoke Hannah, reminding her of what she lacked. "You are worthless!" Peninnah prodded as they walked. "I have God's blessing. Where is yours?"

Each barb from Peninnah reminded Hannah of a promise from Moses's book that blistered against her heavy heart. "Blessed shall be the fruit of your womb" (Deuteronomy 28:4). Children—even with their cries and stubbornness and messiness—had always testified to God's unique and abundant lovingkindness. Why could *she* not drink of that blessing? Why would no child call her *ema* (mother)? She heard only curses, never the one blessing she so desperately longed for.

Broken by Peninnah's taunts and the constant mockery of her own heart, she arrived at God's house, threw her naked pain before the Lord, her faithful God, and cried, "Remember me. Remember your maidservant!" She continued to weep, pleading for the desire of her heart. "O LORD of hosts, if you will indeed look on the affliction of your servant and remember me and not forget your servant, but will give to your servant a son, then I will give him to the LORD all the days of his life, and no razor shall touch his head" (1 Samuel 1:11).

The hot eastern winds blew through the tents, and Eli, the high priest, was tired. Many worshipers had come that day, and sitting on his seat near the entrance, he struggled to stay awake. Not much longer and he could eat his evening meal with his wife and sons. But one woman remained in the outer courtyard, kneeling, facing the Holy of Holies. *What is she doing?* Her mouth moved, but no words came. He scowled at her. "How long will you go on being drunk? Put your wine away from you" (1 Samuel 1:14).

But Hannah had not poured herself wine or hard drink. Her earnest crying, mouthed words, and unspeakable ardor were not the shaky performance of a lush, but rather the desperate pleas of a woman who longed to share her heartache with God.

"No, my lord," she said to Eli. "I am a woman troubled in spirit. I have drunk neither wine nor strong drink, but I have been pouring out my soul before the LORD" (1 Samuel 1:15).

Rebuked, Eli accepted her correction, changed his direction, and blessed her. "Go in peace," he said.

Hannah lowered her head and exhaled. *Peace*—in Hebrew, *shalom*. She heard this word often, spoke it as a greeting, but coming from the priest, it pierced her. She longed for the peace that this word expressed. Peace from the profound depths of God's heart for his people. Peace that sang of completeness, wholeness. Sadly, through the years of her life, Hannah had felt anything but whole. The one gift she longed for never came.

The priest did not stop with *shalom* but added, "The God of Israel grant your petition that you have made to him" (1 Samuel 1:17).

Hannah paused, searched Eli's eyes, and wondered if his words were more than a prayer. *Were they prophetic? A promise that a child would come?* In the end, Hannah knew they were. After years of a silent womb, God's answer came through a bumbled promise from an incompetent priest. And long before any signs of new life whispered within her, joy flooded her soul. She sang, "My heart exults in the LORD; my horn is exalted in the LORD" (1 Samuel 2:1).

Two thousand years later, another woman was plodding along the bleak trail of those suffering with dead wombs. Like Hannah, Elizabeth, John the Baptist's mother, was also the humble wife of a clueless priest. She, too, was past her childbearing years and yet miraculously conceived. And her son's life was also pledged to God, even to his death.

Just as God's gentle yet powerful care of Hannah caused her weeping to blossom into song, from Elizabeth's miraculous pregnancy came great joy. When the angel told Elizabeth's husband about their upcoming pregnancy, he said this: "You will have joy and gladness, and many will rejoice at his birth" (Luke 1:14).

More than just their miraculous pregnancies, Hannah and Elizabeth had another, even more existence-shaking reason for their elation than just the thrill of motherhood. Both their sons, Samuel and John the Baptist, "made straight in the desert a highway" for an even greater baby boy (Isaiah 40:3). Samuel prepared the way first for King David, and through him, the same King who John the Baptist heralded.

Jesus took these women's barrenness and turned their "mourning into dancing...and clothed [them] with gladness" (Psalm 30:11).

Collapse upon the grace of God whose mercy is complete.

STEVE GREEN

Christmas can sometimes bring heaviness, loneliness, and even despair. Like Hannah, bring your sorrow to God and cry out to him. His joy will come.

When has God brought joy out of despair in your life? Currently, what pain or heartache might he be waiting for you to confide in him so he can comfort you with his hope? (Genesis 50:20; Psalm 20:11-12)

Lord God, just as Hannah cried out to you, unwavering in her reliance on your unfailing love, refresh in me the freedom to unburden my heart to you. When sorrow overwhelms me, by your mercy, replace it with joy.

1 Samuel 1:2-11

GOOD CHRISTIAN MEN, REJOICE!

14th century Latin text, translated by John Mason Neale (1818–1886)

Good Christian men, rejoice,
With heart, and soul, and voice;
Give ye heed to what we say:
Jesus Christ is born today;
Earth and heav'n before him bow,
And he is in the manger now.
Christ is born today!
Christ is born today!

Good Christian men, rejoice,
With heart, and soul, and voice;
Now ye hear of endless bliss:
Jesus Christ was born for this!
He hath open'ed heaven's door,
And man is blessed evermore.
Christ was born for this!

Good Christian men, rejoice,
With heart, and soul, and voice;
Now ye need not fear the grave:
Jesus Christ was born to save!
Calls you one and calls you all
To gain his everlasting hall.
Christ was born to save!
Christ was born to save!

16

FOREVER SHEPHERD KING

You were straying like sheep, but have now returned
to the Shepherd and Overseer of your souls.

1 PETER 2:25

As woolen clouds wafted across the moon on a certain night in Bethlehem, the shepherds—a lowly breed, base, unwelcomed by society—remembered their secret confidence, their royal lineage.

A shepherd told his son. "Our father David, he tended his sheep on this very hill."

"King David, abba?"

And the father's face brightened as he repeated the history that echoed through each generation. "Yes, the mighty shepherd king."

"What's that in the sky?"

Centuries earlier, young David's fingers danced freely over his lyre, his love for the Creator soaring to the star-dappled sky. His sheep gently bleated from their fold like his own little choir. He thought of the song Miriam sang when God's people crossed the Red Sea, and Moses's psalm, pleading with God to

"Satisfy us in the morning with your steadfast love" (Psalm 90:14). Comparing their divinely inspired songs to the coughs and bleats of his tired sheep, he smiled to himself. *Well, they're not* exactly *like a choir.*

The breeze carried the aroma of sage bushes, sweetening the sheep's musty stench. Gazing down the mountain, David could see Bethlehem, the town of his birth, marked by the dying light of cooking fires fading to embers. What were his seven brothers doing? Relaxing after their evening meal? He glanced at what he'd packed with him: his jar of olives, bag of dates, figs, almonds. He set down his lyre and leaned back against the sheep gate. He'd rather be *here* than home. Outside in the quiet of the night, he could worship the Shepherd who stirred the songs in his heart.

A rustling snagged his attention, and he scanned the pen's low wall. A stone was jarred from its place. His heart sped. A lamb had wiggled out. Taking stock of the flock, he knew exactly which one was missing—the youngest one, the smallest one, the one who could most easily slip through the cracks. She had been born only a few weeks before, and so he kept a mindful eye on her to ensure the mother was feeding, cleaning, and nurturing her. Being so young, she was perfect prey for lions, bears, and wolves. "Protect your lamb, Lord. Keep her safe from the predators that lurk in the night," he pleaded, an early outcry for deliverance, foreshadowing words he had not yet penned. "Deliver me from my enemies, O my God; protect me from those who rise up against me" (Psalm 59:1).

Leaving the other sheep in the safety of their pen, David grabbed his shepherd's staff and set out to rescue the lost one. He tromped over rocks and weeds, finding the little lamb wandering near a cliff's edge.

A whispered praise, "Thank you, God, for keeping this little one safe," would be echoed years later in his many psalms of worship. "The LORD is good to all; and his mercy is over all he has made…The LORD upholds all who are falling and raises up all who are bowed down" (Psalm 145:9, 14). With gentle skill, he hooked the young lamb with his staff and drew the trembling creature to him. Hoisting her to his shoulders, he returned to the fold—but as he drew near the flock, he heard discordant bleats assaulting the air like the wailing of funeral mourners.

A lion vaulted past him, another lamb in its jaws. David hurried the retrieved lamb safely into the fold, then warriored on sure, quick feet after the predator that threatened his sheep.

He tackled the beast, striking it with a large rock pulled from the ground. When he grabbed the beast's mouth, the sheep fell from its grasp to the safety of the ground. "Go back!" David yelled at the ewe, but she just bleated and watched as David's gaze turned from hers to the predator he was about to fight.

Then, by the moon's light, the eyes of the enraged lion seemed to glow as it released a low growl. Instantly, David lunged forward and grabbed the lion's beard, yanking its head away from him, then pulled his knife and killed the beast (1 Samuel 17:34-35). Years later David's skills—worshiping, shepherding, protecting—would mold him into the greatest of Israel's kings.

But a King was coming who was even greater than David.

Even more intensely than worshiper David, Jesus the worshiper would love his Lord (John 14:31).

Even more tenderly than herder David, Jesus the shepherd would nurture his sheep (John 10:14).

Even more fiercely than warrior David, Jesus the champion would defeat great enemies (Romans 6:5-10; Colossians 2:5).

But a deeper mystery even more clearly defines Jesus's shepherding. "The good shepherd lays down his life for the sheep" (John 10:11). The keeper of sheep who was worshiped in song by myriads of angel choirs that night those lowly shepherds witnessed—that shepherd died willingly for his sheep.

*Jesus and Jesus alone is the shepherd you can
trust, and Jesus and Jesus alone is the one who
can come between you and the wolves.*

TIM KELLER

Dear friends, today, crawl into your Shepherd's arms, confident
in his committed care for you that was bought at a high price.
Remember that Jesus goes to every length so he can ensure the safety
of his vulnerable sheep.

When do you find yourself living as your own shepherd,
made anxious as you try to defend yourself from life's lions?
What personal experiences or verses from Scripture remind you to
trust God as your perfect protector? (Psalm 91:1-6; John 10:27-29;
2 Thessalonians 3:3)

*Shepherd of my soul, as David sang to you, let worship arise from my
own heart. Like the sheep David shepherded, let me follow you. Like
the lambs David guarded, let me rest in your protection. And make
me, dear Father, ready to act as your hands and feet in defending the
vulnerable and providing for the needy.*

Psalm 23

ANGELS WE HAVE HEARD ON HIGH

Traditional French carol, translated by James Chadwick (1813–1882)

Angels we have heard on high,
Sweetly singing o'er the plains,
And the mountains in reply
Echo back their joyous strains.

Refrain:
Gloria in excelsis Deo,
Gloria in excelsis Deo.

Shepherds, why this jubilee?
Why your joyous strains prolong?
Say what may the tidings be
Which inspire your heav'nly song? [Refrain]

Come to Bethlehem and see
Him whose birth the angels sing;
Come, adore on bended knee
Christ the Lord, the newborn King. [Refrain]

17

MEPHIBOSHETH'S SURPRISE

*Having the eyes of your hearts enlightened, that you may
know what is the hope to which he has called you, what
are the riches of his glorious inheritance in the saints.*

EPHESIANS 1:18

Mephibosheth reclined on a sofa on the veranda of his home, enjoying
the spring warmth and gazing at the hills around Jerusalem, rolling with waves
of wildflowers. The view of King Saul's palace, now King David's, brought
back the many hours as a child when he had raced through those halls, hiding from his nurse, jumping onto his father Jonathan's lap, gobbling his favorite meal of lamb and fig and date cake. And those olive trees in the garden.
He'd climbed each one.

A glance at his legs covered by the woolen blanket his childhood nurse had
woven for him reminded him how many changes he'd gone through in his
life. He took a sip of wine from the goblet. His nurse had been there that day.

He had been five years old when his grandfather Saul had gone off one
last time to fight the Philistines. The archers had wounded him, and then he
took his own life. Mephibosheth's father also had died in that battle, bravely,
but that was hardly a consolation to a little boy (1 Samuel 31:1-7). He touched
the ring on his finger, his family's tribe, Benjamin, inscribed on it. Though

memories were foggy, he could see his father's handsome face, his eyes smiling as he put on his armor that morning—the face of a warrior, of a king that could have been. "Don't be afraid," he assured his young son. "Our times are in the hands of the Holy One of Israel."

That day had been the last time Mephibosheth would jump out of bed, scamper through the garden, or climb a tree. Small and frightened, he'd hid in one of those trees on the day that his family had fallen, only for his nurse to find him. "Come down!" she ordered. "We must flee!"

She finally coaxed him off the highest limb, grabbed him in her arms, and ran. In the chaotic flood of soldiers and panicked people, she'd fallen. His feet were crushed, both crippled.

After that, he'd gone to live with a family—not his own—in the house of Ammiel. Mephibosheth shifted in his seat, thinking of Ammiel's name. It meant "my kinsman is God." The name seemed ironic—truly, the only kinsman Mephibosheth had left was the Lord. And not only had he lost a loving family, he was forced to move to one of the most desolate towns in all Israel, Lo Debar, which meant, "No thing."[1] Another irony, for that had been his life—empty, lonely, nothing.

Yet, as he grew, he came to appreciate being so far away from Jerusalem. New kings didn't treat heirs of the former regime well. The thought set Mephibosheth's heart pounding as it had years ago. If King David found him, would he torture, humiliate, or kill him? Probably all. So he had hidden, for many years, until—

"Father!" Mephibosheth's little boy, Mica, came running to the veranda and sat next to him. "It's almost time for you to go to supper."

Mephibosheth smiled. "That's right."

"Why do you always eat with the king?"

"I have told you."

"I know." Mica crawled onto Mephibosheth's lap.

Mephibosheth smoothed his son's scraggly hair. "I don't want to keep the king waiting, but I will tell you one more time—"

"First, he sent his servant to you," Mica interrupted. "Ziba!"

"That's right. We know him well, don't we?"

"Yes. I think he's in the hallway bossing the servants about something."

"He *is* our head servant. He's entitled to do a little bossing."

"Right. But when he first came from King David, you were afraid, because you thought the king had sent him to summon you—to kill you!"

"That's right, because my grandfather had been the king before him." He exhaled. "King Saul treated David very unjustly, even after God sent the prophet Samuel to anoint David."

"But Ziba didn't kill you."

Mephibosheth blinked. "No. I was so surprised! The king said—"

"Do not fear!"

"Yes." Mephibosheth had thought himself to be worthless, a "dead dog." It was still almost impossible to grasp that the great King David cared to even search for him.

Mica snuggled against Mephibosheth's chest. "Because he loved my grandfather, Jonathan."

"He did. Their bond was like no other, and King David wanted to keep his promise to always show God's steadfast love to our family" (1 Samuel 20:14-17).

"He gave you back your land."

Mephibosheth nodded. "But even more kindly, he welcomed me as family."

"And that's why you are always eating your meals with him at the king's table."

"That's right." Mephibosheth scooted to a sitting position and grabbed his crutches. "And as you said, I should be leaving."

"Will he serve lamb?"

"I hope so!"

Jesus's mother Mary's song expresses Mephibosheth's story. "He has brought down the mighty from their thrones and exalted those of humble estate; he has filled the hungry with good things, and the rich he has sent away empty" (Luke 1:52-53).

God's love seeks the weak and builds up the humble. David offered Mephibosheth a seat at his table, and he "always" ate there (2 Samuel 9:13). Every time we partake of the Lord's Supper, we too are dining with the King, welcomed despite our lowly state, given the steadfast love of God displayed, not just in physical food, but in the body and blood of Jesus. "Behold, I stand at the door and knock. If anyone hears my voice and opens the door, I will come in to him and eat with him, and he with me" (Revelation 3:20).

For you have demonstrated the greatness of your power and the kindness of your heart to us. You raised us from the grave of our sin, and gave us a new heart, a new story, and a new future. We feast today, and forever, at your table of mercy and grace. All because of what you've done for us in Jesus.

SCOTTY SMITH

PRACTICE

Mephibosheth always ate at David's table, the perfect example of how we are graciously welcomed to join the Lord Jesus at the Communion table. Next time you partake of the bread and the wine, ponder the great spiritual nourishment of feasting with and on the Lord (1 Corinthians 11:23-26; Luke 22:19-20).

REFLECT

When was the last time you took Communion? How do you reflect on the Lord's body when you receive the elements? (Matthew 26:26-28; 1 Corinthians 11:24-29; Isaiah 53:5)

PRAY

Lord Jesus, without you I am weak, crippled, a "dead dog." Mephibosheth's feet were injured by an unforeseen accident, but your feet were broken by your act of submission to God's will. Even today, your grace, your love, and your scars remain. Yet you have erased my own blemishes and healed my own wounds. You have made me new, whole, transformed. Give me strength to walk with you, bringing your word to a broken world.

READ

2 Samuel 9

SING

AWAY IN A MANGER
Author unknown (1885, 1892)

Away in a manger, no crib for a bed,
The little Lord Jesus laid down his sweet head;

The stars in the bright sky looked down where he lay,
The little Lord Jesus, asleep on the hay.

The cattle are lowing, the baby awakes,
But little Lord Jesus no crying he makes;
I love thee, Lord Jesus! Look down from the sky,
And stay by my cradle, till morning is nigh.

Be near me, Lord Jesus, I ask thee to stay
Close by me forever, and love me, I pray;
Bless all the dear children in thy tender care,
And fit us for heaven, to live with thee there.

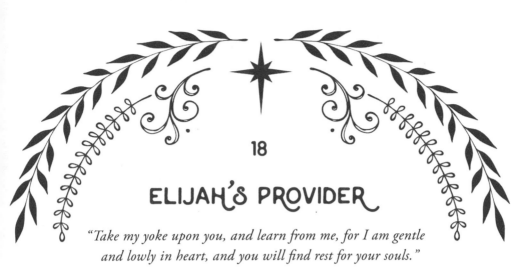

18

ELIJAH'S PROVIDER

"Take my yoke upon you, and learn from me, for I am gentle
and lowly in heart, and you will find rest for your souls."

MATTHEW 11:29

During the time of Elijah...

A rebellious nation. A wicked king. A famine. A war with the
priests of Baal. Drenched sacrifice. Elijah prays. Fire consumes
the altar. Victory! God brings rain. Queen Jezebel threatens. Elijah runs away. Afraid. (See 1 Kings 18.)

"Right here," the weary prophet said to his newly brought-back-to-life
servant,[1] his only companion as he fled the city. "I need you to wait here in
Jezreel."

The young man looked up at Elijah. "But can I not go with you? I'll help
you."

Elijah shook his head. "I go alone."

And so he did, trekking deeper into the isolation of the wilderness. A
day passed—was it only a day? He was too tired to think. Too tired to care.
Finally, he came to a broom tree that gave him blessed shade and concealed
safety, a place where he could rest.

Sitting in the dirt, his back against the tree, he exhaled. His journey was at an end. *Here*, he thought, *I can finally die.* "It is enough; now, O LORD, take away my life, for I am no better than my fathers" (1 Kings 19:4). While he slept, the pre-incarnate Son of God, as the angel of the Lord, came.[2] And when Elijah awoke, the Bread of Life had prepared him bread. The Living Water had given him water. Elijah slept, and after a time, he again awoke to the Lord's touch. "Arise and eat, for the journey is too great for you" (1 Kings 19:7).

Elijah greatly needed the gift of sustenance, for after that, the Lord would call him to travel for forty days and nights. In his own strength, he could not go so long without nourishment, yet the food God had provided satisfied him for the entire journey. Finally reaching the mountain of the Lord, the mountain Moses also climbed (Exodus 19:1-3). Elijah hid in a cleft, waiting, longing for God's presence. *Would the Lord pass by? Would he show himself as he had done to Moses?* (Exodus 33:21-23).

But then, "Behold, the word of the LORD came to him." Yes, the Word of the Lord. "And he said to him, 'What are you doing here, Elijah?'" (1 Kings 19:9).

He spoke his name. And God knew the answer to his question, but still gifted Elijah the time to respond.

The haggard prophet unloaded his heart. He'd been "jealous" to turn the people of Israel back to their God. He'd poured out his life for them, but what difference had all his suffering, his confrontations, his speaking the words God told him to say—what difference had any of it made? All his efforts had failed. Elijah tried casting the blame on God. "The people of Israel have forsaken your covenant, thrown down your altars, and killed your prophets" (1 Kings 19:10).

And so he sat, still frustrated.

But God didn't leave him in that state. "And he said, 'Go out and stand on the mount before the LORD.' And behold, the LORD passed by and a great and strong wind tore the mountains and broke in pieces the rocks before the LORD, but the LORD was not in the wind. And after the wind an earthquake, but the Lord was not in the earthquake. And after the earthquake a fire, but the Lord was not in the fire" (1 Kings 19:11-12).

Elijah yearned for the Lord to be in these earth-shaking events! Didn't the obstinate, ungrateful, idol-worshiping masses deserve a mighty display of God's powerful presence? Hundreds of years before, hadn't almighty God crashed into time through wind, earthquake, and fire right here on this same mountain when giving his Law to Moses? Why was he not now in these things? Where was he?

"And after the fire there was the sound of a gentle whisper" (1 Kings 19:12 NLT).

A gentle whisper. God's power was great and unmatched. He wielded it when his holiness demanded, but in that moment with Elijah, the prophet did not need God's justice, but his grace—the gentle care of his good Father.

Advent comes in a gentle whisper too. "She gave birth to her firstborn, a son. She wrapped him in cloths and placed him in a manger, because there was no guest room available for them" (Luke 2:7). The one who gently whispered to Elijah knew that one day he would come to rest in a manger, to sleep among cows and chickens, a child in a poor family.

And that one still seeks and finds the ones for whom the journey is too great. He touches, feeds, waters, and whispers his love to them—to us.

God uses men who are weak and
feeble enough to lean on him.

HUDSON TAYLOR

God is willing to listen to your complaints, your questions,
even your deepest despair. When the journey is too great for you,
cry out to him. He will gently care for you.

What heartache have you held back from God, whether intentionally
or out of simple forgetfulness? (Psalm 51:6)

Gentle Jesus, I am weary from the long journey of this life.
Feed me, touch me, whisper to me your love,
that I may be renewed to serve once again.

1 Kings 18–19

THE FIRST NOEL
Anonymous 1833

The first Noel the angel did say
Was to certain poor shepherds in fields as they lay,
In fields where they lay keeping their sheep,
On a cold winter's night that was so deep.

Refrain:
Noel, Noel, Noel, Noel
Born is the King of Israel.

They looked up and saw a star
Shining in the east beyond them far;
And to the earth it gave great light,
And so it continued both day and night. [Refrain]

And by the light of that same star
Three wise men came from country far;
To seek for a king was their intent,
And to follow the star wherever it went. [Refrain]

This star drew nigh to the northwest;
O'er Bethlehem it took its rest,
And there it did both stop and stay,
Right over the place where Jesus lay. [Refrain]

Then entered in those wise men three,
Full reverently upon their knee,
And offered there in his presence
Their gold, and myrrh, and frankincense. [Refrain]

Then let us all with one accord
Sing praises to our heavenly Lord,
That hath made heaven and earth of naught,
And with his blood our life hath bought. [Refrain]

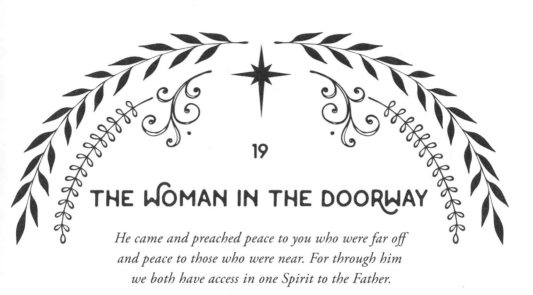

19

THE WOMAN IN THE DOORWAY

He came and preached peace to you who were far off
and peace to those who were near. For through him
we both have access in one Spirit to the Father.

EPHESIANS 2:17-18

One day, Elisha went on to Shunem, where a wealthy woman lived, who urged him to eat some food. So whenever he passed that way, he would turn in there to eat food" (2 Kings 4:8).

The wealthy Shunamite woman stood in the doorway watching the prophet and his servant diminish down the path leading away from her home.

"Why must you always feed that odd fellow?" her husband's fading voice asked.

Closing the ornately decorated door, she turned to her husband. "He's a holy man."

Wealthy, business-savvy, and respected, this woman of stature liked having connections with important people. She settled back into her chair at the table, picked up her goblet encrusted with precious stones, and swirled her deep-crimson wine. She took a sip.

"Holy man of God?" Her husband's wrinkled hands pushed his own chair out from the table. He stood and moved to his more cushioned chair. "His king is not our king. And we don't even worship the same gods as he does."

She stared out the window at the prophet, leaning on his staff as he walked, his servant striding beside him. When they disappeared over the ridge, she glanced at her husband. "Isn't it wise to honor the gods, even the ones not from our own land?"

"Perhaps, but you can't possibly please all the gods." He propped his feet on a footstool, and then relented. "But if you want to cater to the old man, so be it."

"Good." She straightened. "Then tomorrow you will build him a room." She pointed with her eyes. "On the roof."

He peered at her. "A room?"

"Yes, so he can have a place to turn aside to worship when he's here. Place a lamp, a table for bread, and a special chair for him to sit in. It must have real walls. And a bed for him to sleep in."

"Very well."

And so her husband built a beautiful room for the prophet, and when Elisha next passed that way, after a meal, she led him upstairs. "This is for you." She waved her hand into the room but waited outside the door.

Elisha's bushy eyebrows rose. "What is this?"

"Go on," she said.

He entered, viewing the table, the lamp, and the chair. Tears moistened the deep wrinkles beside his eyes. "You have done so much. The Lord will bless you."

She blinked. "I...I have no need."

But she did.

After they left her home, Elisha and Gehazi discussed this woman. "How can we repay her?" Elisha asked. Elisha's servant told him that the woman was barren. Her husband was old, and when he died, she would have no one to care for her.

One day he came there, and he turned into the chamber and rested there.

And he said to Gehazi his servant, "Call this Shunammite." When he had called her, she stood before him (2 Kings 4:11-12).

Her long chiton brushed the steps as she ascended to the roof and waited at the doorway of the prophet's temple-room.

"A son," he said. "This time next year, you will give birth to a son."

She resisted the urge to lay a hand on her stomach and tightened her jaw instead. How could such words emit from his lips? They touched her deepest longing, her most vulnerable ache.

In this moment her heart struggled to believe that this old man, who ate at her table, worshiped and slept in her upper room, was truly more intimate with the gods than any other professed holy man. "No, man of God," she said. "Do not lie to me." She respected his traditions and practices, even embraced some of them, but a God who could create a child from the nothingness of her dead womb? No. The prophet was lying. A cruel lie.

And yet, the next year, around the time Elisha had prophesied, she did bear a son. Perhaps Elisha's God was not merely one of many but actually the one true God. Perhaps she *could* trust him.

"One day when her child was older, he went out to help his father, who was working with the harvesters" (2 Kings 4:18 NLT). Before the harvesters had gathered their first bundle, the boy came running to his father, crying in pain. "Oh, my head! My head!"

A servant carried him through the fields to his mother. She held him on her lap, her fingers threading through his hair, until the sun rose high and oppressive in the sky. At noon, her long-awaited little boy died.

A raven cawed overhead, casting a shadow on her as she gazed heavenward. She hadn't asked for this gift of a child, but she loved him. As she wept, she remembered the long-ago flutters in her womb, his coos, giggles, even his tantrums. Yes, in each breath of his life, she'd loved him.

Now, the love that clasped her to him instead compressed her heart, hardening it into stone. She had thanked Elisha's God. Began to believe. And what had happened? Her beloved boy's cold limp body slumped in her arms. She never should have trusted Elisha or his God. The prophet must answer for this.

Her body wracked with grief, she lifted her only son's body and carried him up the stairs to Elisha's room. Opening the door, she paused in the doorway to study the candle, the table, and the chair. She hadn't crossed the threshold before. It was the prophet's place of worship and rest, not hers. But now, she took a breath and slowly stepped inside. With gentle care, she laid her son's body on the bed and covered him. Then she stepped out, closed the door, saddled a donkey, and departed to find Elisha.

She found him on Mount Carmel and threw herself at his feet, weeping.

Elisha's servant Gehazi tried to pull her from the prophet, but she wouldn't let go.

"Leave her alone," Elisha said. "She is in bitter distress" (2 Kings 4:27).

"Then she said, 'Did I ask my lord for a son? Did I not say, 'Do not deceive me?'" (2 Kings 4:28).

So Elisha sent Gehazi ahead to lay the prophet's staff over the boy's face in an attempt to revive him.

But the woman refused to leave unless Elisha went with her, so he arose and followed her. When they arrived, he left her, entered the room, now a tomb, alone.

Waiting outside the room, the woman wept silently. Would Elisha bring her son back to her? Could his God—could any god—breathe life into a corpse? Eventually, she heard movement. Could it be…? Then, what was that? A sneeze? That was her son's sneeze! Altogether she heard seven sneezes, and then Elisha opened the door. Her son was alive!

"Thank you, Elisha!" And she fell at his feet, overwhelmed with gratitude.

Catching her breath, she stood, engulfed her son in her arms, and went out.

The wealthy woman never asked for a son, but God blessed her. Then she lost her boy, only to get him back again.

Mary never asked to bear the Son of God, but God blessed her. Then Mary lost her boy, only to get him back again.

In both of these women's stories, God opened the door for them to experience his love in and through intense suffering. As both entered in, both found blessings beyond their imaginings.

Love (III)

Love bade me welcome. Yet my soul drew back
Guilty of dust and sin.
But quick-eyed Love, observing me grow slack
From my first entrance in,
Drew nearer to me, sweetly questioning,
If I lacked any thing.

GEORGE HERBERT

Compare this excerpt from Herbert's poem to Song of Solomon 5:6. "I opened to my beloved, but my beloved had withdrawn himself" (KJV). "Bade" is past tense of "bid," and in Herbert's time was pronounced like "bad."

PRACTICE

Admitting the one thing she desperately needed would've made her vulnerable, but she needed a son. We all need a Son.

We often put on a happy face and hide our deepest hopes and needs from God—and even from ourselves. Today, be vulnerable with the Lord by acknowledging an unmet longing you might be hesitant to admit—whether it's comfort from pain, deliverance from trauma, refuge from loneliness. Trust in his power and step through the threshold into his extravagant love, believing full-heartedly that he is capable of the impossible.

What keeps you from entering this threshold? When have you placed limits on God's power or love that kept you from asking him for something you felt was impossible, or for something you felt you didn't deserve? Conversely, when have your expectations for your own self-sufficiency held you back from admitting you need help? (Psalm 84:11; Matthew 7:11; Luke 1:37)

Dear Father, even though your love infuses every crevice of my life, I still often stand outside the door as if I'm not your child. As you called the Shunamite woman to enter in, let me cross the threshold of your love, trusting like Mary in your goodness.

2 Kings 4:18-37

O COME, DIVINE MESSIAH

M. l'abbé Pellegrin; translated by Sister Mary of St. Philip (1877)

O come, divine Messiah;
The world in silence waits the day
When hope shall sing its triumph
And sadness flee away.

Refrain:
Dear Savior, haste! Come, come to earth.
Dispel the night and show your face,
And bid us hail the dawn of grace.
O come, divine Messiah;
The world in silence waits the day
When hope shall sing its triumph
And sadness flee away.

O Christ, whom nations sigh for,
Whom priest and prophet long foretold,
Come, break the captive's fetters,
Redeem the long-lost fold. [Refrain]

You come in peace and meekness
And lowly will your cradle be;
All clothed in human weakness
Shall we your Godhead see. [Refrain]

20

A QUEEN'S ENTRANCE

Let us then with confidence draw near to the throne of grace,
that we may receive mercy and find grace to help in time of need.

HEBREWS 4:16

Sunlight broke through the slits in the meager walls of the home where Hadassah had lived since she was a child. Today, she would become a bright bloom in the radiant bouquet of girls presented at the palace of the Persian Empire's king, hoping that perhaps the mighty ruler would find favor in her, choose her to be his new queen.

Hadassah picked up a pistachio from the wooden bowl beside her, and then set it back down. She couldn't eat. Her thoughts spiraled around the king, hungering for a new queen. Surely it would not be her. She touched her simple dress, glanced down at her worn sandals. Most likely, she would be confined to live in his palace for the remainder of her life as one of a myriad of concubines, never allowed to marry or have a family of her own.

A family of my own. Soon she would say goodbye to her only family—Mordecai. Her older cousin was like a father to her, had been her only family since her Abba and Ema died when she was young. Mordecai, who had strolled through the market with her on so many warm afternoons, choosing apricots, lemons, artichokes, and sometimes lamb for the evening meal.

Mordecai, whose aging hands dried her wet cheeks when she cried. He had also taught her that God kept his hand on the Israelites—that he had chosen them among all nations of all the earth to be his own.

Soon she would say goodbye to him.

As usual, Mordecai had been up and out early, talking with the other men at the city gates. Hadassah now heard his footsteps approach, and then the front door opened, letting in the cool morning air, carrying with it the scent of pomegranate blossoms.

"Hadassah." He took her hands in his cool, rough ones. "Are you ready?" He paused to look at her, seeming to take her in. Then he chuckled. "I think I'm the one who is not ready for you to leave this place."

She fell into his arms. "Mordecai…thank you for all…"

"No need to thank me." He pulled back and wiped her tears with his thumb. "They are waiting," he said. "The girls are gathering near the gates."

As they approached the other girls, Mordecai whispered one last command. "Don't speak of your people or kindred," he instructed. "It may not be safe."

She nodded, then let go of his hand. He promised to go to the palace every day.

Upon arriving, she gave up her name, Hadassah, for a Persian one, Esther, which meant "star." She was placed under the command of Hegai, the king's chamberlain, the keeper of the girls. Esther heeded Hegai's every instruction. For a year, she learned what to wear, how to apply her makeup with exquisite artistry, how to walk with modest elegance, what to say and not say, how to please—all for the king.

And Hegai's counsel bore fruit. Esther delighted the king more than any other woman, and he chose her as his new queen. Esther—an orphaned Jewish girl once called Hadassah— would become a queen.

A queen who obeyed her king. A pang of worry twisted in her stomach. Esther couldn't forget what had befallen the previous queen. She had disobeyed. And now she was no longer queen.

True to his word, Mordecai hovered near the palace, checking on her, watching, listening.

Mordecai did not obey like Esther. One day, as Mordecai stood near the palace, the king's highest official, Haman the Agagite, rode by on his chariot. All were required to bow before this man. As dust from his horses' hooves stirred, the king's servants around him bowed before this powerful man. But Mordecai refused to bow, standing alone. Day after day, he refused to bow.

Finally, Haman stopped his chariot. "You!" he said. "The king's servants tell me that you do not bow when I ride by. Why do you disobey the king's edict?"

"I am a Jew," he explained. "I cannot bow to any but the Lord."

In a fury, Haman plotted revenge, not just against Mordecai but against all Jews. He proposed an edict ordering that all Jews would be put to death. When he slyly presented it before the king, the king sealed it with his signet ring. Irreversible.

"When Mordecai learned all that had been done, Mordecai tore his clothes and put on sackcloth and ashes, and went out into the midst of the city, and he cried out with a loud and bitter cry" (Esther 4:1).

In the haven of the palace, Esther had been isolated from news of the edict. When her ladies told Esther about Mordecai's lamenting, she sent a messenger to him, and soon learned of the edict to kill all Jews. Her cousin called on her to approach the king to seek his help. But how could she? The law stated that if anyone—even the queen—entered the king's presence without being summoned, he or she must wait and see if the king would raise his scepter. If the king didn't, the person would be killed.

But Mordecai persisted. "For if you keep silent at this time, relief and deliverance will rise for the Jews from another place, but you and your father's house will perish. And who knows whether you have not come to the kingdom for such a time as this?" (Esther 4:14, paraphrase).

When she heard Mordecai's words from the messenger, she made a decision. She would enter the king's throne room. She sent a message to Mordecai,

"Go, gather all the Jews to be found in Susa, and hold a fast on my behalf, and do not eat or drink for three days, night or day. I and my young women will also fast as you do. Then I will go to the king, though it is against the law, and if I perish, I perish" (Esther 4:16).

Fear gripped the Hebrews all over the land as they fasted alongside Esther and her ladies. On the third day, dressed in royal robes—as the queen she had become—she entered.

"And when the king saw Queen Esther standing in the court, she won favor in his sight, and he held out to Esther the golden scepter that was in his hand. Then Esther approached and touched the tip of the scepter" (Esther 5:2).

Queen Esther didn't die, and through her act of courage the Jews survived.

A great deal of time and money went into preparing Esther to be fit to wear the garb of a queen. The king would never have approved of Hadassah, an Israelite girl living in poverty, but dressed in royal garb, he saw her beauty, and saw that—after all her training, and baths, and perfumes, and fittings—she was the very essence of a queen.

In contrast, Jesus left his royal throne and became a servant in order to save the rebellious people he loved so dearly. In our human state, we could never approach his throne, so our King took on pauper's clothes so that we might one day wear the fine robes befitting sons and daughters of the most high King.

I entered the throne room where Jesus, my Lord,
Was waiting the captive to free;
He reached out His sceptre; He spake the glad word,

And cleansing and joy came to me.
O glory! O glory, what rapture is mine!
The King in His beauty I see;
I'm singing His praises since Jesus divine
Extended His sceptre to me.

REV. HENRY J. ZELLEY

His scepter of grace is raised to you, so go in.
Bring your requests, talk to him, delight in simply being near him.
He won't turn you away.

Whether you pray at specific times every day, write out your prayers in a journal, go on prayer walks, or use a devotional to prompt your prayers, which prayer habits are most enriching to your walk with God? Which prayer habits would you like to try out? What is one way you can make coming before the Lord a more consistent part of your daily life? (Philippians 4:6; Romans 8:15; Song of Solomon 2:10)

Beloved Jesus, I approach your throne, not fearfully but boldly.
Hear my cries and help me to live as your bride.

Esther 3–5

O COME, ALL YE FAITHFUL

Latin hymn, attributed to John Francis Wade (1751),
translated by Frederick Oakley (1841)

O come, all ye faithful,
Joyful and triumphant,
O come ye, O come ye to Bethlehem;
Come and behold him
Born the King of angels;

Refrain:
O come, let us adore him,
O come, let us adore him,
O come, let us adore him,
Christ the Lord.

God of God, Light of Light;
Lo, he abhors not the Virgin's womb:
Very God, Begotten, not created. [Refrain]

Sing, choirs of angels;
Sing in exultation,

Sing, all ye citizens of heaven above;
Glory to God in the highest. [Refrain]

Yea, Lord, we greet thee,
Born this happy morning:
Jesus, to thee be glory given;
Word of the Father,
Late in flesh appearing. [Refrain]

21

ISAIAH'S PLEA

*Though your sins are like scarlet, they shall
be as white as snow; though they are red as
crimson, they shall become like wool.*

ISAIAH 1:18

Sitting on the roof of his Jerusalem home, Isaiah watched silently as dawn threaded along the dusty horizon. Memories of that time when he entered God's throne room replayed through his mind in unimaginable images. The throne. The smoke. The Lord, high and lifted up. His robe filling the temple. His voice shaking its foundations.

And the song of the six-winged seraphim, *Holy, holy, holy.* Over and over and over again. He glanced up at the sky, its apricot hues deepening as dawn widened. Even now, did seraphim voices echo around the throne of their great God? *Surely they must.*

"Woe is me," he said aloud, as he had to the Lord and seraphim. "I am a man of unclean lips." He had cursed himself, for a curse he deserved. Abiding even for a moment in the presence of the Holy One—he was undone, torn apart, as good as dead.

Yet one of the seraphim had placed a burning coal from the altar on his unclean lips. "The coal from God's altar took my guilt away," he reminded himself. "The coal from God's altar atoned for my sins." The coal suggested sacrifice, but he had witnessed no animal sacrifice in the throne room of God. So whose sacrifice was it? (See Isaiah 6:1-7 for Isaiah's vision of God's throne room.)

His own name, Isaiah, which meant "God is salvation," whispered the answer.

Only one could save. Only one.

Carts rattled along the stone streets as early morning merchants hauled their goods to market. The prophet glanced toward the king's palace. Here in David's capital, David's palace had been inhabited by many kings since the country split into two kingdoms—Israel to the north, and Judah to the south, where Isaiah resided.

Most kings had not done what was right in the eyes of the Lord. He who ruled from Judah's throne now, Ahaz, worshiped false gods, engaged in degenerate practices, and offered children to be sacrificed on pagan altars. And his wicked example influenced his people, God's treasured possession, to live no differently than those in the moral abyss around them.

Outside Judah's borders, two enemy nations lusted for the land of Israel. Ahaz had trembled like trees shake in the wind when he heard this.

Isaiah's son, named A Remnant Shall Return, (Shear-jashub) approached his father on the roof. "Today, Father?" he asked. "You said we must talk to the king."

"Yes." The prophet pulled his child to his side, horrified to imagine how King Ahaz could have sacrificed any child to the pagan idol. "The Lord has commanded us to go to the Washer's Field."

"Washer's Field?" His son's eyebrows rose.

"A depraved place, I know. But God commanded us to go there. He knows where the king may be found." They ate a morning meal, and a few hours later, together they left their home.

When they reached the field, they found the king sitting in a shaded chair, surrounded by attendants. Smoke from a fire filled the air as animals were offered before the images of Baal that King Ahaz had himself commissioned. Musicians played the lute and the harp in odd harmonies. A small group of women danced. Priests chanted prayers to the deity.

"He doesn't deserve mercy," A Remnant Shall Return whispered to Isaiah. "Why would God offer to help him?"

Isaiah touched his own lips. "Because he is abundant in steadfast love," he assured his son.

Approaching the king on his chair, Isaiah bowed. "Your majesty, the Lord has sent me with a message for you. This is my son, A Remnant Shall Return."

Color abandoned the king's face. "What are you saying, Isaiah?" He scoffed. "Where shall a remnant return from? We yet live in our own land. And I have secured a plan to keep us here." He eyed his advisor, whose robes were soiled from their filthy rituals. "I have an alliance, unknown to you. Our old friends, the Egyptians, are going to fight with us."

The Egyptians? Oh, Lord! But Isaiah laid aside his frustration so he could continue speaking God's message to the king. "The Lord has called me to tell you, O king, 'Be careful, be quiet, do not fear, and do not let your heart be faint'" (Isaiah 7:4). He watched the king's expression. "You need not faint because of these two nations."

The king lowered his head and glared like a provoked dog. "I am not afraid. I told you, I already have a plan to ward off our northern neighbors. And I also have additional means of ensuring our security." He pointed at the fire, burning before the image of Baal. "We seek Baal's help—and he will give it!"

Isaiah shook his head. "Ask a sign of the LORD your God; let it be deep as Sheol or high as heaven" (Isaiah 7:11).

King Ahaz's lips twisted into a sneer. "I wouldn't think of putting my God to the test."

Isaiah crossed his arms. *Feigned piety before a pagan altar? Is nothing too low for this king?* "If you will not ask, then you are refusing his help. Your alliance with the godless Egyptians will fail. A greater army will come and defeat Judah. All in the land will be taken to captivity. That will be your legacy, but believe me, O king, God will not forget his people."

Isaiah and A Remnant Shall Return pivoted and began to leave, but God placed a fresh promise upon his prophet's lips. "He has another word for you, Ahaz." *Though you don't deserve to hear it.*

"You are testing my patience."

"Since you did not ask for one, the Lord himself will give you a sign."

"Fine. Let's hear it."

"Behold, the virgin shall conceive and bear a son, and shall call his name Immanuel" (Isaiah 7:14).

Ahaz laughed out loud. "A virgin shall conceive? Absurd!" And "Immanuel? Who would name their child God." He peered at his advisor who was also smirking. "God with us?"

The coming Savior was first promised in the garden where the rebellious Adam rejected God's blessing in favor of his own pride-filled desire. In the beloved Isaiah 7:14 passage, the coming Savior was promised again, this time in a field where the despicable Ahaz also rejected God's blessing in favor of his own way. But this time, God's plan was emerging in more clarity. For the first time, he revealed that this deliverer would be born of a virgin.

The holiness of God teaches us that there is only one way to deal with sin—radically, seriously, painfully, constantly. If you do not so live, you do not live in the presence of the Holy One of Israel.

SINCLAIR FERGUSON

PRACTICE

Identifying, acknowledging, and confessing our sins ignites untold growth in our lives. Ask God to reveal your sin to you and enter the painful yet fruitful process of repentance, knowing his great love washes you as white as snow.

REFLECT

In what areas do you leave God's blessings behind and choose your own way? As Ahaz used idolatry and even false piety to justify his waywardness, what masks do you use to avoid confronting your own disobedience? (Isaiah 53:6)

PRAY

Preferring to stay hidden in the false safety of my self-deceiving lies, I perceive only the faintest shade of my sin. Search my heart, O God, and grant me courage to grapple with my own darkness. Jesus, please cleanse my lips with the burning coals of your sacrifice, that I may sing "holy, holy, holy" to the only one worthy of praise.

READ

Isaiah 6–7

SING

LO, HOW A ROSE E'RE BLOOMING

German hymn, ca. 1500, Stanzas 1-2 translated by Theodore Baker, 1894; Stanzas 3-4
translated by Harriett R. Spaeth, 1875; Stanza 5 translated by John C. Mattes, 1914

Lo, how a Rose e'er blooming
From tender stem hath sprung!
Of Jesse's lineage coming
As men of old have sung.
It came, a flower bright,
Amid the cold of winter
When half-gone was the night.

Isaiah 'twas foretold it,
The Rose I have in mind:
With Mary we behold it,
The virgin mother kind.
To show God's love aright
She bore to men a Savior
When half-gone was the night.

The shepherds heard the story,
Proclaimed by angels bright,
How Christ, the Lord of glory,
Was born on earth this night.
To Bethlehem they sped

And in the manger found him,
As angel heralds said.

This Flower, whose fragrance tender
With sweetness fills the air,
Dispels with glorious splendor
The darkness everywhere.
True man, yet very God,
From sin and death He saves us
And lightens every load.

O Savior, child of Mary,
Who felt our human woe;
O Savior, King of glory,
Who dost our weakness know,
Bring us at length we pray,
To the bright courts of heaven
And to the endless day.

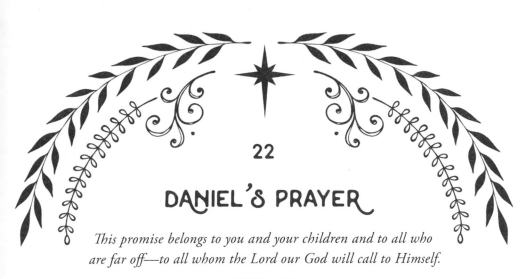

22

DANIEL'S PRAYER

This promise belongs to you and your children and to all who are far off—to all whom the Lord our God will call to Himself.

ACTS 2:39

Daniel grinned as he entered the outer court of the palace. He'd served three kings since first being dragged from his home to Persia by her invading armies. The Lord had been patient, but eventually, his justice came down against Israel's and Judah's sin. Both now lived in exile, away from the promised land.

King Nebuchadnezzar had assigned Daniel to be chief of the magicians. As a result of his privileged position, he'd been able to train many young men in the ways of his God. How many, he couldn't recall. And how far had those teachings spread? This was probably not what Nebuchadnezzar had in mind when he assigned him the job.

Nebuchadnezzar was no longer king, and now Darius, a man graced with the gray hair of experience, currently ruled Babylon. But it was one of this king's satraps, so-called "protectors of the realm," that now met Daniel outside the throne room. The deceit in this corrupt young man's heart was unmasked through his smirk as he unrolled the scroll. "Whoever makes petition to any god or man for thirty days, except the king," the satrap stated, his gaze piercing

Daniel, "shall be cast into the den of lions." This man knew of Daniel's practice of calling upon his God. This hateful edict was clearly directed at him.

His long life of continually seeking the Ancient of Days for guidance had created in Daniel an instinct. When a conflict arose, even one targeting his faith, what else would he do but pray? So, he exited the palace and embarked on the fifteen-minute trek home to his prayer sanctuary. A weeping willow's dappled shadows splaying over the sidewalk told Daniel evening was approaching. He prayed at this time every day.

Daniel shook his wrinkled head as he strode beside the tranquil Euphrates River. Boats—fishing, transport, trade—floated in a serene parade displaying Babylon's wealth. But his mind wandered from the river to the lion pit.

Daniel glanced at the age spots on his hands. Now? Now they plotted against him? He remembered the prophet Jeremiah's words (Daniel 9:2). If he understood the Scriptures correctly, only a few more years and God's purpose for the exile would be complete. Restoration, return, even revival would follow. After all these years, would God allow him to die before seeing the glorious day when he could again walk the land where Abraham walked, where King David ruled in glory?

He saw himself as a child, gazing at the hills surrounding Jerusalem, speckled with sheep and their shepherds. The busy music of the marketplace. He paused walking, closing his eyes for a moment. The temple. A tear sprung as it always did when the image of Solomon's magnificent structure invaded his thoughts. The unthinkable had happened, Nebuchadnezzar had burned the temple to the ground. Would it ever be rebuilt?

Thirty days—could he cease praying for thirty days? Wouldn't he be able to serve God better alive? He arrived at his house and walked upstairs, knelt in front of the open window, and prayed toward Jerusalem, toward the symbol of God's presence. No, he could not go one day without praying, much less thirty.

And so, in due time, the satraps caught sight of him "making petition and plea before his God," and reported his disobedience (Daniel 6:11). When King Darius realized it was his signature that convicted Daniel, he was distraught. Darius knew Daniel had done nothing wrong other than to have fallen into his own corrupt satraps' plot. Daniel had served with integrity in the midst of the many corrupt in his government. Darius labored the whole day long to find a way to rescue Daniel, but the law of the Medes and Persians could not be revoked (Daniel 6:8). No one could change these laws. There was nothing even the great king of all the Persian Empire could do. Daniel would die.

At sunset Daniel was thrown into the lions' den. A stone was rolled over the mouth of this place of death, to keep him from escaping or being freed. And it was sealed with the king's ring.

The stone. The seal.

Mourning, Darius didn't sleep, but rose at break of day to run to the lions' den. Daniel would be dead, the den, a tomb. In anguish, the king cried out, "O Daniel, has your God delivered you from the lions?"

"O king, live forever!" (Daniel 6:21).

How relieved was the king to hear this formal greeting! Daniel was not dead, but alive!

"God sent his angel and shut the lions' mouths," Daniel said, "and they have not harmed me, because I was found blameless before him; and also before you, O king, I have done no harm" (Daniel 6:22).

Not guilty. All the years he served in Babylon, all the teaching he imparted to the magicians, enchanters, Chaldeans, and astrologers about his God was true. Daniel was vindicated. And God, through the pattern of this event, foreshadowed a certain event to come.[1]

The king rejoiced.

"I make a decree, that in all my royal dominion people are to tremble and fear before the God of Daniel, for he is the living God, enduring forever; his kingdom shall never be destroyed, and his dominion shall be to the end" (Daniel 6:26-27).

In the land of exile, God's light shone.

"Wait and watch," Daniel had told the magi he trained. "The Son of Man will come. A sign will come."

So they waited and watched the skies. Finally, after 600 years a star appeared in the inky black canopy above. And they knew it was the sign Daniel had foretold.

"Now after Jesus was born in Bethlehem of Judea in the days of Herod the king, behold, wise men (magi) from the east came to Jerusalem, saying, 'Where is he who has been born king of the Jews? For we saw his star when it rose and have come to worship him'" (Matthew 2:1-2).

Christ for the world, for the world needs Christ!

ERIC LIDDELL

"Where is he who has been born King of the Jews?"
the magi asked Herod when they sought him (Matthew 2:1-2).
They called him the Jewish king, yet these Gentiles, these offspring
of Daniel's disciples, longed to worship him. When Jesus hung on
the wretched-glorious cross, a sign with those same words,
"The King of the Jews," hung over his head (Matthew 27:37).
Yet he was never king to only one people, but to any who call on
him. In what way does your perspective change when considering
life in this world, knowing Christ is King? He is your King too.
Worship him today.

Where were you when you first "saw the star"? In other words, share the story of how you came to know the Savior. (Psalm 66:16)

God of wonder, you called me from afar and made me your own.
Use me, like Daniel, to spread the truth of your love.

Daniel 6

WE THREE KINGS OF ORIENT ARE
John H. Hopkins (1857)

We three kings of Orient are;
Bearing gifts we traverse afar,
Field and fountain, moor and mountain,
Following yonder star.

Refrain:
O star of wonder, star of light,
Star with royal beauty bright,

Westward leading, still proceeding,
Guide us to thy perfect light.

Born a King on Bethlehem's plain,
Gold I bring to crown him again,
King forever, ceasing never,
Over us all to reign. [Refrain]

Frankincense to offer have I;
Incense owns a Deity nigh;
Prayer and praising, voices raising,
Worshiping God on high. [Refrain]

Myrrh is mine; its bitter perfume
Breathes a life of gathering gloom;
Sorrowing, sighing, bleeding, dying,
Sealed in the stone-cold tomb. [Refrain]

Glorious now behold him arise;
King and God and sacrifice:
Alleluia, Alleluia,
Sounds through the earth and skies. [Refrain]

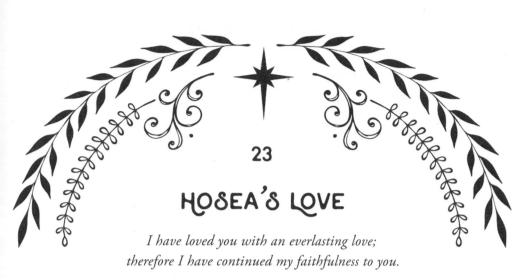

23

HOSEA'S LOVE

I have loved you with an everlasting love;
therefore I have continued my faithfulness to you.

JEREMIAH 31:3

As they walked along the desert trail, Hosea gazed at his son Jezreel's murky gray eyes, so similar to Gomer's, his beloved wife, who had once again run away.

"Why are we going to the spring?" Hosea's second born, No Mercy (Lo-ruhama) asked, her wavy brown hair bouncing as she trotted beside him.

"Because it's hot!" Jezreel answered. "And slow down. You're going to ruin your sandals."

"There it is!" Not My People (Lo-ammi), the youngest, pointed toward a sandstone cave. "Gideon's cave."

A sparkling spring flowed from its creviced walls into a large glassy-clear pool. Olive trees, palm trees, and lush bushes also adorned the area, a burst of life in the copper-colored wilderness.

"That's right," the prophet said. "The water will feel good on my parched throat." He wiped a line of sweat from his temple.

"I'm going to slurp like Gideon." Not My People cupped his dusty hands to his mouth and stuck his tongue out.

"Ugh, please don't put those grimy fingers so close to your mouth," Jezreel scolded.

A mixture of sage, palm, and licorice scents wafted to Hosea's senses as they arrived at the spring. He and his children satisfied their thirst by cupping the water in their hands—despite Jezreel's rebuke—like Gideon's small army (Judges 7:5-6). Before the three children could race away to explore the cave or climb a tree, Hosea stopped them.

"Come." He moved toward an olive tree, its compact leaves providing a broad canopy of shade. "Enjoy the cool relief the Lord has provided through this good tree." He reclined under it, and the children scooted next to him. No Mercy laid her head on his lap.

Not My People pouted. "I want to sit next to Abba!"

"There's room for both of you." Hosea patted his other leg, and Not My People folded in next to him.

"What's going on, Abba?" Jezreel asked, his forehead tense. "Is it Ema?"

At Jezreel's words, each child's face hazed over. These little ones had experienced more disappointment from their absent mother than any children should. Hosea placed a hand over his own heart. He, too, had been devastated. Repeatedly. But it hurt the children most of all.

"I'm sorry." Hosea's voice faltered. "She has left again."

"Of course!" Jezreel stood. "She always does. I don't know why you keep letting her return."

Hosea patted his son's arm, coaxing him to sit back down. "I let her return for one reason, son."

No Mercy wiped a tear from her cheek. "You love her?"

Yes, he loved her. Adored, cherished, delighted in—not enough words. How he longed to woo her, to speak tenderly to her, to be a husband of faithfulness to her. But she ran. She always ran.

"Why did she leave?" Not My People asked.

Hosea glanced up at a tall, stout palm tree, its fronds stretching like eagles' wings. The children followed his gaze. "Imagine if that mighty tree believed it was unloved, ugly, worthless."

"Not *that* tree," No Mercy said.

"It's beautiful, isn't it?" Hosea patted his daughter's head. "And so is your Ema. She's my beloved wife, but she doesn't remember who she is."

The children sat quietly.

"Do you know who you are?" Hosea asked the children after a moment.

"I know God gave us these names." Jezreel tossed a rock into the spring. "Mine means, 'God sows,' and it's the name of that valley—" he pointed past the cave. "The Valley of Blood, where lots of people died, and the people worshiped idols."

Hosea nodded. "That is true. The Jezreel Valley will face God's judgment." He glanced at the others. "What about you two?"

"I'm No Mercy. That's what the Lord named me, and I know why."

The youngest jumped on a rock then back down. "He named me Not My People." He peered at his sister. "And I know why too."

"Let's allow the oldest to tell us this time." Hosea nodded at Jezreel.

"The names aren't about us. He used them to send a message to Israel." He looked at his father for approval.

"And why would God give you such names?" Hosea prodded.

"Our names are warnings that if the people don't trust the Lord, they will be hurt," No Mercy answered. "He wants to bless them, but when they worship other gods, they are saying they don't want his blessing. He loves them, like you love Ema. So much."

"That's right. And you are his children, as you are mine."

"Yes, Abba," Not My People said. "Can we play now?"

"Say it first."

Two doves fluttered above, and then soared down to the water's edge. The children smiled.

"Go ahead," Hosea said, his eyes on the doves. "Say the promise God gave me."

Together they quoted, "I will sow her for myself in the land" (Hosea 2:23).

"That one's for Jezreel." Not My People interjected. "His name means, 'God sows.'"

"Yes, yes. Continue."

They quoted, "And I will have mercy on No Mercy, and I will say to Not My People, 'You are my people'; and he shall say, 'You are my God'" (Hosea 2:23).

"That's good news, isn't it?" Hosea smiled at each child.

They nodded, and then the two little ones ran off, but Jezreel lingered behind. "What are you going to do about Ema? Do you know where she is?"

"Yes, son."

"The slave market?"

"That's right." Hosea's throat tightened. "I will go purchase her." With all the money he had.

Three infants were given peculiar names that sent a message of warning to God's bride. It was as if God were saying to Israel, "Come back to my love. Don't let these be your real names. This is not who you are!" God promised to reverse the curse that Gomer's children's names forebode, but how could he when his bride was enslaved by the vicious master of sin? A price had to be paid for her release.

And a price had to be paid for our release (1 Peter 1:18-19; Matthew 20:28; 1 Corinthians 6:20).

One infant was born who, because of his love for us, took on Hosea's children's names:

Jezreel—Jesus entered into the valley of blood by shedding his own blood for the sins of his people (Romans 5:9).

No Mercy—the most merciful Lord Jesus received no mercy, but instead the wrath of God when he died on the cross (2 Corinthians 5:21, 1 Peter 2:24).

Not My People—Jesus, the Holy Son of God, was forsaken by his Father, taking on the rejection his people deserved (Mark 15:34).

Because he knew that we—we like Gomer—would repeatedly squander his blessings and turn to lesser lovers, he purchased our freedom for a far higher cost than Hosea's treasure.

God loves each of us as if there were only one of us.

SAINT AUGUSTINE

If you trust in Jesus, you are his bride, beloved, chosen.
He delights in you. You are not worthless. You are not alone.
You are his. Trust him. Believe him.

What keeps you from remembering that you are precious to Jesus?
(Ephesians 3:19)

My Lord, you gave me mercy when I was "No Mercy."
You called me yours when I was "Not Your People." You gathered the
scattered bits of my fractured heart. And you bought me. You bought

me with the highest price of your own Son. Yet, I doubt your love. I run from you. Chase me, O Lord. By your grace, let me know, to the depths of who I am, your great, eternal, never-ending love.

Hosea 1–3

IN THE BLEAK MIDWINTER

Christina Georgina Rossetti (c. 1872)

In the bleak midwinter
Frosty wind made moan,
Earth stood hard as iron,
Water like a stone:
Snow had fallen,
Snow on snow, snow on snow,
In the bleak midwinter,
Long ago.

Our God, heaven cannot hold him,
Nor earth sustain;
Heaven and earth shall flee away
When he comes to reign:
In the bleak midwinter
A stable place sufficed

The Lord God Almighty,
Jesus Christ.

Enough for him whom cherubim
Worship night and day,
A breastful of milk
And a mangerful of hay:
Enough for him
Whom angels fall down before,
The ox and ass and camel
Which adore.

Angels and archangels
May have gathered there,
Cherubim and seraphim
Thronged the air,
But only his mother,
In her maiden bliss,
Worshiped the Beloved
With a kiss.

What can I give him,
Poor as I am?
If I were a shepherd,
I would bring a lamb,
If I were a wise man
I would do my part,
Yet what I can I give him,
Give my heart.

24

MICAH'S TOWN

God chose what is foolish in the world to shame the wise;
God chose what is weak in the world to shame the strong.

1 CORINTHIANS 1:27

I will pray on the mountain," the prophet Micah decided when he awoke once again to the nation's sin. He packed a small bag and headed out without delay.

Weaving through the crowded streets of Jerusalem, he attempted to avoid the filth threatening to tarnish his bare feet. Years earlier as a barefoot child in a quiet farming town, he had romped not through streets but in and out of meadows and streams. Back then, his free toes displayed a child's unfettered joy. Now he chose to go out with bare feet and scarce clothes to symbolize the despair weighing down his heart like a millstone.

To his left, a fortune teller's call stirred him from his memories. She stood in her shabby booth, the scent of burning incense reminiscent of a pagan temple. A poor woman approached the mystic, two children clinging to her legs. All three wore black veils, one widow and two fatherless children. The woman wanted to know if her hopes would come true—if a kinsman would rescue them from starvation.

The fortune teller put on a smile. "When you sacrifice to the gods, they will favor you," she said, before accepting the woman's payment.

Micah walked on and spotted a "holy man" in priestlike robes. He sat in a booth made of polished wood and fine linen. Carvings of many gods hung from the wall as well as small scripts of the Hebrew Scriptures. The holy man was talking to another man whose shoulders drooped as if he hadn't slept in days.

"The magistrate took your house?" the holy man asked.

"Yes. I was current on my payment, but the lender demanded the balance all at once. When I couldn't pay, he brought soldiers to drive us out."

"You poor man." The holy man's eyes slanted with faux sympathy. "I will say a prayer for you, but I'm afraid even one like me, dedicated to helping the unfortunate, have but scant means. Spare a shekel for the prayer?"

Micah's stomach churned. Shameful. Reaching the edges of town, he strode past lavish villas where men sat on sunlit verandas drinking wine poured by slaves and devising new plans to fill their stables with horses, their bellies with food, their coffers with money.

The city stank, and Micah was glad when he passed through the gate into the foothills surrounding Jerusalem. But a day of walking led him to another tainted city—Samaria in the Northern Kingdom of Israel. With its multitudes of idols, Samaria was just as corrupt as Jerusalem. Finally leaving both cities behind and reaching Mount Carmel, the tension in Micah's shoulders lightened.

An evening wind carried brooding clouds that huddled around the mountain's stony peak. Step by step Micah climbed, nearly tripping over roots and rocks hidden beneath the sage bushes, until he reached a flat, secluded spot to set up camp.

Micah wandered to a boulder overlooking Samaria and the fields that surrounded it. Jerusalem lay even farther beyond. The rolling hills and valleys sprawled before him, starred by hearth fires that marked the presence of those who occupied the land. Micah let the evening cool him, breathing in the peace that came with rising above the chaos below.

With each step on his journey, Micah had planned what he would say to the Lord once he settled on the mountain, but now that he was here, his words dissolved into tears. He wept for the widow and her family, for the man who had lost his home, for the many who had been exploited by the unethical upper class. Both Israel's and Judah's greatest cities should have been springs of mercy, justice, and humility, but they had forfeited these treasures and turned against the God who loved them.

From his stone seat, Micah poured out his soul in lament. As the evening loomed, the Lord answered his cries by giving him a message as dark as the night's shroud that encircled him.

"The LORD is coming out of his place," God told Micah, "and will come down and tread upon the high places of the earth. And the mountains will melt under him, and the valleys will split open" (Micah 1:3-4).

Melting mountains. Split valleys. Clearly the Lord would not withhold his judgment against the unjust forever. In silence, Micah continued to listen, his surroundings dimming in the brilliance of the Lord's words.

God explained that the great city of Samaria would become a "heap in the open country," and her idols would be "beaten to pieces" (Micah 1:6-7). Jerusalem too would become a "heap of ruins" (3:12). God told Micah to tell the rulers: "Hear this, you heads of the house of Jacob and rulers of the house of Israel, who detest justice and make crooked all that is straight, who build Zion with blood and Jerusalem with iniquity...Zion shall be plowed as a field" (Micah 3:9-10, 12).

This image struck him, transporting him to the fields of his father's farm after plowing. Empty, desolate, dry. Instead of thriving growth, only dirt remained, as if the crops had never existed. To imagine Israel and Judah, the nations he loved, crumbled to nothing...

He gazed at the softly lit cities. "How far have God's people fallen!"

Yet, the Lord only sent judgment because his compassionate eyes saw the pain those in power inflicted on the poor. Micah trusted that the destruction of these mighty cities would be just, but he still mourned the consequences of their downfall. What about the oppressed in those cities?

The Lord comforted him. He would not ignore the hurting. "I will assemble the lame and gather those who have been driven away and those whom I have afflicted; and the lame I will make the remnant, and those who were cast off, a strong nation; and the LORD will reign over them in Mount Zion from this time forth and forevermore" (Micah 4:6-7).

But God didn't leave this promise open-ended. He gave Micah an even more specific detail about how the message of God's love would spread to the nations. The promised king and Savior of the downtrodden would come to a humble, insignificant town. A little town. And God told Micah the exact one it would be.

"Where is he who has been born king of the Jews?" the magi asked the king of Judea, Herod the Great. "For we saw his star when it rose and have come to worship him."

This news troubled King Herod. A new king? Herod couldn't have that. He ordered the chief priests and scribes to come to him.

"Where?" he demanded. "Where will this king be born?"

They told him, "As it says in the prophet's book, 'But you, O Bethlehem, from you will come forth for me one who is ruler of Israel, whose coming forth is from of old, from ancient days'" (Matthew 2:1-6; Micah 5:2).

"*Bethlehem?*"

The Bible experts of Herod's time knew where the Messiah would be born. It had been foretold to the prophet Micah 700 years before! But why did the great king Jesus choose to arrive in meek, simple Bethlehem? Because like Bethlehem, Jesus would be humble. He would rescue his oppressed people by walking dusty streets, eating with sinners, making friends with the lowly. He found the hurting where they were. He came to them. He comes to us.

I see his tree, with blossom on its bough,
And nothing can be ordinary now.

GEORGE HERBERT

Micah 6:8 provides a clear, specific model for believers to practice. Write down ways you can live out this verse in your life.

He has told you, O man, what is good;
and what does the LORD require of you
but to do justice, and to love kindness,
and to walk humbly with your God?

REFLECT

Micah was burdened by the injustice he saw around him. Our world is also plagued with inequity, oppression, and untold suffering. What are some specific areas of injustice that you can bring before the Lord? (Job 5:8-16; Psalm 94:15-16; Luke 18:1-8)

Who is a God like you, pardoning iniquity and passing over transgression for the remnant of his inheritance? He does not retain his anger forever, because he delights in steadfast love.
(Micah 7:18)

Micah 5

O LITTLE TOWN OF BETHLEHEM
Phillips Brooks (1868)

O little town of Bethlehem,
How still we see thee lie;
Above thy deep and dreamless sleep
The silent stars go by:
Yet in thy dark streets shineth
The everlasting light;
The hopes and fears of all the years
Are met in thee tonight.

For Christ is born of Mary;
And gathered all above,
While mortals sleep, the angels keep

Their watch of wondering love.
O morning stars together
Proclaim the holy birth;
And praises sing to God the King,
And peace to men on earth.

How silently, how silently
The wondrous gift is given!
So God imparts to human hearts
The blessings of his heav'n.
No ear may hear his coming,
But in this world of sin,
Where meek souls will receive him still,
The dear Christ enters in.

O holy Child of Bethlehem,
Descend to us, we pray;
Cast out our sin, and enter in,
Be born in us today.
We hear the Christmas angels
The great glad tidings tell;
O come to us, abide with us,
Our Lord Emmanuel.

25

SIMEON'S LIGHT

The people walking in darkness have seen a great light; on those living in the land of deep darkness a light has dawned.

ISAIAH 9:2 NIV

The elderly prophetess knelt near the entrance to the inner court of the temple. Since her husband had died so many years ago, she never left the temple. She'd spent many nights in prayer and worshiping and fasting. She grasped her aching back and straightened. She'd only been married seven years when he had died, but since then she hadn't been alone. Her years serving the Lord had provided a life richer than a queen. As she turned to sit down, she spotted her old friend walking toward her amid the temple workers performing their morning tasks. "Simeon, come."

Simeon's gaze skipped around as he hurried closer. Spry for his age, Anna thought, but especially spirited this morning.

"Shalom, Anna," he said as he approached her. "Have you…" His voice softened, and he glanced at the entrance, "…seen anyone?"

"Simeon." Anna patted the stool next to her. "Sit. What's causing this unrest in you?"

Tentatively, the aged man took his seat. "It's…" A mysterious grin lifted the corners of his mouth. "I can't speak it. I think…Maybe," his shoulders relaxed, "the Spirit of God led me here today."

"Well, I'm sure he did," she said. "Why wouldn't he want you to come to the temple on this day, or any day?" She eyed her sleeping mat and meager belongings, and lowered her voice. "Or night."

Simeon stood, stared at the entrance, then sat back down.

"What is it, friend?" Anna asked.

Simeon let out a shaky breath and almost spoke, but then held back. He had never shared his deepest hope with her. Countless years earlier, as he was desperately praying, the Holy Spirit had told him he would not see death before he saw the Messiah.

"O Anna, have we not waited all these long years?" he finally said. He tapped his foot against the temple floor, counting the seconds going by. "I thought maybe today…." He glanced toward the small crowd of worshipers entering the temple for midmorning prayers.

"Oh, friend." She placed a hand on her chest. "Would that he did come today." She tilted her ancient head. "But we don't know. It could be one hundred years."

"Sooner than that, I think."

Anna paused, studying his face, but Simeon said nothing, so she continued. "Many before us also waited. Think of our first parents—Adam and Eve. Before anyone else, they received the promise. The serpent would be crushed by the Savior."

Simeon nodded. "Yes, and the Redeemer, too, would be crushed, but not completely."

"Only his heel," Anna finished Simeon's thought. "And think of Noah. He could've been the deliverer, but…"

"A great man—if God hadn't hidden him safe in the ark, none of us would be here."

"But he fell to temptation. He was not the Messiah." Anna glanced toward the Holy of Holies. "Moses."

Simeon clasped his hands together. "Moses! Deliverer, yes. God's great favor rested on him, did it not? Ten plagues, the Red Sea, the holy Law, water from the rock—" He shook his head. "He shouldn't have struck the rock."

"No."

"And it wasn't even David—a man after God's own heart."

"All those beautiful psalms."

"But not David." Simeon imagined the prophet Nathan's discouragement when David fell into great sin. "By then it must have seemed like an eternal age had passed."

"After David, our fathers' and mothers' disobedience spread like weeds, strangling the truth." Anna's voice cracked. "Unfaithful leader followed unfaithful leader."

"With a few flashes of hope. Don't forget Elijah and Elisha. They raised those boys from the dead! I would've thought either one of them was the Messiah."

"Yes, and there was Josiah, Esther, Daniel, the prophets." A dove suddenly swept in from the outer court. It must have escaped its cage. It circled and then flew out again.

The two elderly saints, wearied from talking, sat silently on their chairs as the hours passed. Watching, waiting. Shadows fell. Evening was coming. The temple gate would soon close.

Anna's eyes rounded as she looked at Simeon. "Maybe not today…"

A man led a lamb toward the altar, handed it to the priest.

And then, a couple strode in, simple clothes, poor. The woman held a child in her arms, close to her heart. The husband carried a cage with two turtledoves. Eying the altar where sacrifices were made, the mother's gaze tarried for a long moment.

The husband gently placed his hand on the mother's back, guiding her. As they walked toward them, Simeon looked at Anna. Her gaze locked with his. Tears were already streaming down her cheeks. They knew. They both knew. They were finally seeing the one who was promised before the beginning, the seed of the woman, the God who sees, the joy of the barren—Emmanuel, God with us.

Simeon took the child in his arms and sang. "Lord, now you are letting your servant depart in peace, according to your word; for my eyes have seen your salvation that you have prepared in the presence of all peoples, a light for revelation to the Gentiles, and for glory to your people Israel" (Luke 2:29-32).

Sleeper awake, the darkness was a dream
For you will see the Daypring at your waking,
Beyond your long last line the dawn is breaking.

MALCOLM GUITE

PRACTICE

Merry Christmas! As you walk through this day, in all you do, give thanks to the long-awaited Savior for the gift of his coming.

REFLECT

What aspects of Christmas give you the most joy?
(Philippians 2:5-8; John 1)

*Dear Jesus, as Simeon and Anna rejoiced at your coming,
may I always revel in the gift of you.*

Luke 2

JOY TO THE WORLD
Isaac Watts (1719)

Joy to the world! The Lord is come:
Let earth receive her King;
Let every heart prepare him room,
And heav'n and nature sing.
And heav'n and nature sing
And heav'n and heav'n and nature sing

Joy to the earth! The Savior reigns:
Let men their songs employ;
While fields and floods, rocks, hills, and plains
Repeat the sounding joy,
Repeat the sounding joy,
Repeat, repeat the sounding joy.

No more let sins and sorrows grow,
Nor thorns infest the ground;
He comes to make his blessings flow
Far as the curse is found,
Far as the curse is found,
Far as, far as the curse is found

He rules the world with truth and grace,
And makes the nations prove
The glories of his righteousness,
And wonders of his love,
And wonders of his love,
And wonders, wonders of his love.

NOTES

Chapter 4: Abraham's Rest

1. Michael Horton, "Covenant," Ligonier.org, November 1, 2011, https://www.ligonier.org/learn/articles/covenant; Bruce K. Waltke, *An Old Testament Theology* (Grand Rapids: Zondervan, 2007), 310.

Chapter 5: Hagar's Cry

1. "The Angel of the LORD," Ligonier.org, September 6, 2006, https://www.ligonier.org/learn/devotionals/angel-lord.

Chapter 9: Judah's Fear

1. Since Judah takes the lead, I thought it would be interesting to imagine this story through his eyes. Be sure to also read the biblical passages.

Chapter 10: Jochebed's Ark

1. In Exodus 2:2, the Hebrew word describing the child is *tov*, which means good, pleasing, fair to the sight. God uses *tov* to describe creation after each day in Genesis 1. *Strong's Concordance,* s.v. "ṭō·wḇ," entry 2896, https://biblehub.com/hebrew/tov_2896.htm.

Chapter 11: Israel's Bread

1. Michael Card, *Inexpressible: Hesed and the Mystery of God's Lovingkindness* (Downer's Grove: IVP Books, 2018), 9-13. This whole book is an unfolding of the word *hesed* throughout the Bible, but pages 9-13 give a concise yet detailed explanation of the little word's multifaceted meanings.

Chapter 13: Manoah's Wonder

1. The ESV translates it "wonderful," but that word is so common in our language that it doesn't put enough emphasis on the wonder of it. ("Why do you ask my name, seeing it is wonderful?") The man of God's name was beyond their understanding.

Chapter 14: Naomi's Son

1. ESV Reformation Study Bible, note on Ruth 2:20, https://www.biblegateway.com/resources/reformation-study-bible/Ruth.2.20.

Chapter 17: Mephibosheth's Surprise

1. Heb. *lô dĕḇär H4274* [with variant spellings], by popular etymology, "nothing." (Zondervan Illustrated Bible Dictionary, as found in Bible Gateway https://www.biblegateway.com/passage/?search=2+samuel+9&version=ESV

Chapter 18: Elijah's Provider

1. Some commentators suggest Elijah's servant was the boy he, by God's strength, raised from the dead. See 1 Kings 7:17-25.

2. "The Angel of the LORD," Ligonier.org, September 6, 2006, https://www.ligonier.org/learn/devotionals/angel-lord.

Chapter 22: Daniel's Prayer

1. Did you see it? An unjust verdict, a "tomb," a stone, a seal. Distraught friend running there at the break of day…

Hymns Used

1. Great Commission, *Trinity Hymnal: Red Cover Edition.* (Suwanee, GA: Great Commission Publications,1990)
2. "Go, Tell it on the Mountain—The Story Behind the Song", December 20, 2012, https://gaither.com/go-tell-it-on-the-mountain-the-story-behind-the-song/
3. "The First Nowel the Angel Did Say" https://hymnary.org/text/the_first_nowell_the_angel_did_say
4. "O Come, Divine Messiah" https://hymnary.org/text/o_come_divine_messiah
5. "We Three Kings of Orient Are" https://hymnary.org/text/we_three_kings_of_orient_are
6. "In the Bleak Midwinter" https://hymnary.org/text/in_the_bleak_midwinter

HYMNS USED

Unless otherwise noted, all hymns have been taken from
Trinity Hymnal: Red Cover Edition[1]

1. **Of the Father's Love Begotten**
   Translation by J. M. Neale (1851), extended by Henry W. Baker (1861)

2. **Comfort, Comfort Ye My People**
   Johannes Olearius (1671); translated Catherine Winkworth (1863)

3. **See Amid the Winter Snow**
   Edward Caswall (1858)

4. **Silent Night**
   Joseph Mohr (1816); translated John Freeman Young (1859)

5. **What Child Is This?**
   William Chatterton Dix (1865)

6. **Come, Thou Long-Expected Jesus**
   Charles Wesley (1744)

7. **Who Is This So Weak and Helpless?**
   Walsham How (c1888)

8. **O Come, O Come, Emmanuel**
   Latin antiphons (12th century), Latin hymn (1710), translated by John
   Mason Neale (1851)

9. **While Shepherds Watched Their Flocks**
   Nahum Tate (1700)

10. **Go Tell It on the Mountain**[2]
    African American spiritual, stanzas John W. Work III (1907)

11. **It Came Upon a Midnight Clear**
    Edmund H. Sears (1849)

12. **God Rest Ye Merry, Gentlemen**
    English Traditional Christmas Carol (17th Century)

13. **In Emmanuel's Land** (The Sands of Time Are Sinking)
Anne R. Cousin (1857) based on Samuel Rutherford, (1600–1661)

14. **Once in Royal David's City**
Cecil Frances Alexander (1848)

15. **Good Christian Men, Rejoice**
14th century Latin text, translated by John Mason Neale (1818–1886)

16. **Angels We Have Heard on High**
Traditional French carol, translated by James Chadwick (1813–1882)

17. **Away in a Manger**
Author unknown (1885, 1892)

18. **The First Noel**[3]
Traditional English carol, 17th century

19. **O Come, Divine Messiah**[4]
M. l'abbé Pellegrin; translated by Sister Mary of St. Philip (1877)

20. **O Come, All Ye Faithful**
Latin hymn, attributed to John Francis Wade (1751), translated by
Frederick Oakley (1841)

21. **Lo, How A Rose E're Blooming**
German hymn, ca. 1500, Stanzas 1-2 translated by Theodore Baker,
1894, Stanzas 3-4 translated by Harriett R. Spaeth, 1875, Stanza 5
translated by John C. Mattes, 1914

22. **We Three Kings of Orient Are**[5]
John H. Hopkins (1857)

23. **In the Bleak Midwinter**[6]
Christina Georgina Rossetti (c. 1872)

24. **O Little Town of Bethlehem**
Phillips Brooks (1868)

25. **Joy to the World**
Isaac Watts (1719)

RESOURCES

So many resources exist to help us study the Bible. As a special Advent gift, I thought I'd share a few tools that have made studying the Bible a bit easier for me.

 PODCASTS

Help Me Teach the Bible, with Nancy Guthrie, by the Bible Coalition

> An episode on every book of the Bible with amazing Bible teachers who are experts on that particular book.

Forty Minutes in the Old Testament, with Chad Bird and Daniel Emery; *Thirty Minutes in the New Testament*, with Erick Sorensen and Daniel Emery, by 1517

> Verse by verse, the hosts walk through the Bible, giving detailed understanding of the text as well as the original languages.

WEBSITES

Bible Hub

> My favorite feature of this Bible website is its easy access to an interlinear Bible. If you need to look at the Hebrew or Greek, it's super easy to click on the link. Once you're there, you can jump to the Hebrew or Greek dictionary.

Bible Gateway

> I use this Bible website for access to its considerable list of study Bibles, commentaries, Bible dictionaries, and Bible encyclopedias for a minimal subscription fee.

BOOKS

Waiting on the Word: A Poem a Day for Advent, Christmas and Epiphany by Malcolm Guite (Canterbury Press Norwich, 2015)

> Malcolm Guite's collection of poems is as insightful and heart-encouraging as his own poetry.

ACKNOWLEDGMENTS

I've been working on this book, in a way, for twelve years! When my four kids were little, we joined a homeschool co-op called HIS Ministry Co-op. I don't know why I was so blessed, but I was gifted with the amazing honor of teaching Bible class to middle schoolers for most of those years. Teaching the Bible compelled me to study it as I never had before. How can I ever adequately thank HIS Ministry Co-op for that amazing gift? Teaching at HIS is not only the soil from which this book sprouted, but my study of the Bible sustained me through some intensely difficult years, constantly refocusing my eyes on the one the Bible is all about—the Lord Jesus.

I must thank my family next. You were so gracious to cook meals, give me time to write, and cheer me on all along the way. I love each of you so very much.

I'm also grateful to some spectacular critique partners. Thank you, Jan Anderson, for your nudges toward a deeper level of poetry and theological precision. Deborah Anderson, for reading those early chapters and encouraging me to keep on. And especially to my dear friend Katherine Scott Jones for her faithful Monday meet-ups that scrubbed my words, organized my stray threads, and encouraged my heart.

To Reverend Mark Collingridge, thank you for the time and effort you've invested in my biblical training over the years! And for steering me down an accurate path in areas of doctrine—I really appreciate it. Reverend Matt Barker, thank you for your time and encouragement in reading this manuscript for me.

All those I've worked with at Harvest House have been more than kind, professional, and Christ-centered. A special thanks to Emma Saisslin—I couldn't be more grateful. And to Steve Laube, my agent. You're the best.

And finally, one last mention—my gratitude to The Rabbit Room. I used several of the quotations you all so graciously suggested on your Facebook page. Thank you!

ABOUT THE AUTHOR

Ocieanna Fleiss has written several books including her memoir, *Love Like There's No Tomorrow*. She taught the Bible for more than a decade, always delighting in how God's love is shown throughout his Word. Ocieanna and her husband have four kids and make their home in Washington State. Visit Ocieanna.com

To learn more about Harvest House books and
to read sample chapters, visit our website:

www.HarvestHousePublishers.com

HARVEST HOUSE PUBLISHERS
EUGENE, OREGON